Luxury Sales Force Management

Luxury Sales Force Management

Strategies for Winning Over Your Brand Ambassadors

Michaela Merk

palgrave
macmillan

First published 2014 by
PALGRAVE MACMILLAN

Palgrave Macmillan in the UK is an imprint of Macmillan Publishers Limited, registered in England, company number 785998, of Houndmills, Basingstoke, Hampshire RG21 6XS.

Palgrave Macmillan in the US is a division of St Martin's Press LLC, 175 Fifth Avenue, New York, NY 10010.

Palgrave Macmillan is the global academic imprint of the above companies and has companies and representatives throughout the world.

Palgrave® and Macmillan® are registered trademarks in the United States, the United Kingdom, Europe and other countries.

ISBN 978–1–137–34743–5

This book is printed on paper suitable for recycling and made from fully managed and sustained forest sources. Logging, pulping and manufacturing processes are expected to conform to the environmental regulations of the country of origin.

A catalogue record for this book is available from the British Library.

A catalog record for this book is available from the Library of Congress.

Typeset by MPS Limited, Chennai, India.

Contents

Conclusion / **194**

List of Tables, Figures and Illustrations

Tables

Figures*

Illustrations

---

* All figures have been designed by Michaela Merk.

Foreword

The relationship between the brand and its sales force is like the relationship between family members – a blood bond. It is the duty and the challenge of top management to humanize the brand so that it becomes dear to every salesperson's heart. The brand has to generate pride in belonging and passion among its team in order for the organization to expand and succeed. The sales force is like a rugby team: unified in its purpose, keen on developing the best winning strategies, always preparing to fight its best fight.

No brand can sustain or develop in the long run without a strong sales force willing to fight for it. Of course, the quality of the product is essential, as well as maintaining the motivation and pride of the sales force, but the challenge lies in continually maintaining such motivation and pride. Routine is the enemy of sales and, consequently, of the brand. Routine should never prevail. The sales team are the lungs of the brand; marketing and finance are the heart and the brain. Without air, the lungs can't breathe, the heart and the brain stop, and the brand dies.

Successful salespeople need to be rewarded immediately. If rewarded, they continue to excel and keep on striving to improve their own performances. There should be a certain degree of competition among salespeople, and yet the cohesion and unity of the team should be preserved. The salespeople who love their brand will do everything they can to put it on the winning podium …

Alain Dominique Perrin

Non-Executive Director at Richemont Group, former President of Cartier International, President of EFMD (European Foundation for Management Development) and President of EDC (École des Dirigeants et Créateurs d'Entreprises)

Key contributors to this book

Bader, Natalie, CEO of Prada France, former President at Fred International, former Marketing Director at Sephora

Banessy Monasterio, Nathalie, General Manager at Ercuis, former Managing Director at Escada France, Retail Director at Descamps, Retail Development Director at Richemont

Bassène, Paul, High Jewelry Manager at Cartier

Blanckaert, Christian, Professor in Luxury Management at ESCP Europe and former CEO of Hermès Sellier and Hermès International

Breguet, Emmanuel, Brand Manager of Breguet France and in charge of the brand's heritage

Cazorla, Elisabeth, President of Jacadi

Champey, Jean-Charles, former Store Manager at Yves Saint Laurent

Combes, Combes, Training Director at Chanel, former International Training Director at Guerlain

Coumau, Coumeau, General Manager of Editions de Parfums Frédéric Malle

De Bary, Shayda, Store Manager at Sonia Rykiel, former Store Manager at Dries Van Noten and Miu Miu

Egiziano, Eric, Headhunter at Lincoln Associates

Fauvet, Alexandre, former Executive Vice President at Lacoste

Ferragu, Alexandre, former Retail Sales Manager Luxury and Accessories at Printemps

Grodzicki, Lawrence, Demandware Project Management Director, former E-commerce Project Manager and Retail Systems Expert at Timberland

Guten, Michel, Sup de Luxe President, Vice President Comité Champs-Élysées, former Vice President of Cartier

Laromiguière, Pierre, President of Baobaz

Lasvigne, Verena, Senior Spa Director at Four Seasons Hotels and Resorts

Leprince-Ringuet, Elodie, International Retail Director at Robert Clergerie, former European Retail Director at Bonpoint

Nemarq, Alain, President of Mauboussin

Perrin, Alain Dominique, Non-Executive Director at Richemont Group, former President of Cartier International, president of EFMD (European Foundation for Management Development) and President of EDC (École des Dirigeants et Créateurs d'Entreprises)

Pollet, Elodie, Brand Creator and CEO of Eutopie

Radmilovitch, Christian, Digital Expert and Consultant

Rodriguez, Raphael, professional dancer, coach and former sales associate at Repetto

Roger, Corinne, Retail and Human Resources Director at Patrick Roger

Sabathé, Sandrine, Sales Representative at Lancôme

Smadja, Brigitte, Van Cleef & Arpels Store Manager

Vallanet-Delhom, Marie, President of the Van Cleef & Arpels School

Vidal, Arnaud, former Vice President Watches and Jewelry at Ralph Lauren and former General Manager of Audemars Piguet

Acknowledgments

This book is not only based on my own management experiences but also on the research results I obtained during my PhD, which I completed in 2012 at the Sorbonne Graduate Business School. I wanted to use the findings of my extensive qualitative and quantitative research and transform them into a hands-on management book.

I will therefore begin by thanking Géraldine Michel, Marketing Professor at IAE Paris, who was my thesis advisor and guided me with great professionalism throughout all stages of my work. She enhanced my understanding of academic research and used her brand expertise to strengthen my approach as a professional. This collaboration showed me that both worlds were complementary and greatly influenced each other.

My deepest thanks also go to Alain Dominique Perrin, Non-Executive Director of Richemont Group, with whom I had an in-depth exchange about sales force management strategies. He had been quoted by so many sales associates, store managers and directors during the course of my interviews that it became clear I had to meet him and understand his unique management style. I feel honored that he agreed to write the Foreword of this book.

I would also like to thank Stéphanie Janique, consultant at my agency, Merk Vision & Partners, who has supported me at every stage of this book and who encouraged me to go on to write it immediately after the completion of my PhD. When you want to accomplish a book like this, it is priceless to have someone with whom you can share your thoughts and who contributes to the genesis of such an important work at each stage of the process.

I also owe a big thank you to the entire Palgrave Macmillan team who trusted me and believed in my ability to develop a book of this size and depth in the short time given. I want to express particular thanks to Eleanor Davey Corrigan (for being my first contact and coordinator), to Tamsine O'Riordan (who succeeded Eleanor and accompanied me throughout the entire publication period), her assistant Josephine Taylor, and Jamie Forrest for all their marketing support and not to forget Elizabeth Stone for her amazing work during the entire production process.

I also want to thank Michel Gutsatz, CEO of Scriptorium Company, who introduced me to this fabulous team.

Luxury Sales Force Management could not have been conceived without the input of hundreds of top managers and salespeople working for premium and luxury brands. I would therefore like to give my special thanks to all these salespeople for their warm welcome into their highly luxurious stores and for always treating me as a very special guest. Without your anecdotes, stories, experiences, thoughts and emotions this book could not have been produced. You provided the foundation of this work, you inspired me by your words, you filled my heart. In addition, I want to thank all the visionary CEOs, retail, training and human resources managers who spent precious time answering my questions and openly shared with me their secrets for successful sales force management.

I am grateful to the representatives of numerous luxury brands and corporations such as Audemars Piguet, Cartier, Dior, Editions de Parfums Frédéric Malle, Fendi, Fred, Guerlain, Jacadi, Lacoste, Lancôme, Longchamp, Marionnaud, Mauboussin, Miu Miu, Patrick Roger, Prada, Printemps, Repetto, Richemont, Robert Clegerie, Sephora, Sonia Rykiel, Tiffany, Van Cleef & Arpels and many more for all their valued contributions.

When interviewing salespeople, I realized that the most passionate among them talked in metaphors, using numerous images. Therefore, I wanted to bring life to this book by illustrating the most striking anecdotes the salespeople had shared with me. Many thanks to the talented Albert Dessinateur for his wonderful, straight-to-the-point illustrations, which perfectly translated my observations.

It is impossible to write a book on management and retail without having acquired a lot of experience beforehand. I therefore want to thank my previous employers, L'Oréal, Marionnaud and Estée Lauder, who allowed me to manage, coordinate and motivate hundreds of salespeople. They enabled me to develop my understanding of two worlds: the brand and the retail universes. Without these concrete experiences, I would not have had the initial insight that made me realize the importance of establishing a relationship between the salespeople and their brands, nor would I have been able to compare my own vision with the results of the interviews I conducted among managers and salespeople.

I also want to thank my parents and my sister who have always been a great support, encouraging me to continue to strive for my goals and never give up.

Finally, I would like to express my gratitude to all those who spent precious time reading the book and gave me feedback before publication, in particular Anne Losq and Judith Dada, my precious trainee at Merk Vision & Partners.

You all managed to win over my heart, and give me the encouragement I needed to produce this work!

Author's Note

It is my strongest belief that salespeople's performance is any brand or retailer's key to success. Salespeople, especially in service-driven industries such as luxury, stand directly between the customer and the brand and its products. They therefore can have a strong influence on a brand's life cycle in either a positive or negative way.

Throughout my professional career, in management positions at premium brands and retailers, I always had the impression that because a great deal of money was being spent on advertising campaigns much of the focus was on building brands or on better understanding the customers' purchasing habits. Salespeople always seemed to be the last element in the company to be considered. I was told many times not to involve the sales force in decision-making processes or to refrain from asking their opinion in order to avoid chaos: "They sell, we decide."

This often made me feel angry and sad, since I recognized the fact that salespeople had a great deal of experience due to their daily contact with the customers and with the realities of business. They are the ones living with the brand every day, standing in stores representing them on a daily basis.

Both the brands and the retailers have the opportunity to ignite real passion in the hearts of salespeople, to light their fires. In short: a brand can only last for decades when members of its sales force establish strong relationships with the brand they sell.

At many stages in my career I noticed a need for this, starting from the time when I was a salesperson myself, many years ago, representing selective cosmetic brands for L'Oréal in the French market, driving from fragrance store to fragrance store for names such as Helena Rubinstein, Biotherm or Lancôme.

As a product manager, still within L'Oréal's Luxury Division, my task was to prepare product launches and to present the new items to the sales force every six weeks. The more strongly I managed to ignite their passion for the new product, the more they identified with the brand and the higher the sales in the end. In order to do this, I had to leave my comfort zone, be creative and surprise them every time.

Years later, as general manager and retail director for the professional makeup brand Bobbi Brown within the Estée Lauder Group, I directly managed a large team of salespeople. Besides managing the brand, I had to represent it in the name of its creator, Bobbi Brown. Becoming a role model and the brand's biggest ambassador for an entire team was a wonderful but challenging experience. In order to fully embody the brand I was trained in the USA by the brand creator herself and her team. The better I understood the brand's philosophy, the better I could live the brand myself and transmit the flame of passion to those in the field.

And finally, as category director for the perfumery chain Marionnaud/ A. S. Watson, my role was to make hundreds of salespeople excited about all the new brands and products I decided to integrate into our portfolio. Here, too, I could see that a constant effort was needed to stimulate the motivation of salespeople, by strengthening their relationships with the brands they were selling.

The question of winning over salespeople's hearts became so important to my thinking and actions when managing brands and sales associates myself that I wanted to shed more light on this topic. It is such a relevant subject for all brands and retailers today, but prior studies have barely considered it. I therefore examined the "mysterious" relationship between the sales force and the brand in the context of my three-year PhD. During this period and afterwards, while preparing this book, I interviewed over 600 salespeople working for luxury and premium fashion, accessories, cosmetics, fine food as well as watch and jewelry brands, predominantly in France but also in Germany, the UK and the USA. The interviewed salespeople are or were employed by selective service-driven brands. They either worked in the brand's own stand-alone boutique, at a concession in a department store, represented the brand in interaction with multi-brand retailer salespeople, called sales representatives, or they directly worked for multi-brand retailers.

Even though these sales channels differ from each other considerably in terms of sales strategies and customer structure, the results of my inquiries showed no significant differences in the relationship patterns between salespeople and the brands they were representing.

After qualitative research in the field, I continued my study by interviewing top managers such as retail directors, training managers, human resources directors and general premium and luxury brand managers. This twofold approach allowed me to identify different visions, mindsets, gaps, desires and strategies. It also enabled me to discover whether managers had the same vision of heart-winning management as their sales teams.

As CEO and founder of the strategic consulting and training agency Merk Vision & Partners, which focuses on the premium and luxury industries, I could already successfully implement the findings of these studies by accompanying selective brands in their development through executive training and consultancy sessions, as they launch in international markets and as they enter into the digital world. In my company, all our efforts are directed toward strengthening the salesperson's loyalty and relationship with the brand.

This book should serve as an eye-opener, inspiration and action tool for managers who want to know how to win their salespeople's hearts, how to strengthen lasting ties with the brand they represent, and how to light the fire of salespeople's passion and keep it burning!

Introduction

Strengthening the Relationship between the Sales Force and their Brand is a Must, Not a Choice!

How can you expect customers to establish strong relationships with your brand if your own salespeople have not built close bonds beforehand? As soon as the customers enter your stores, they come into contact with salespeople. Ideally, your sales force should be your brand's true ambassadors, representing it in both their appearance and their actions. This encounter with your sales force is usually the only human contact a customer gets in any interaction with your brand. If salespeople play their part well, such an encounter can be memorable and full of emotion. It is generally the only time in the customers' experience when they have a personification of the brand – for instance, Mr. Armani or Mrs. Prada, in front of them. They can breathe in the brand spirit, hear about its mystery and touch its creations. This is when they will learn all they want to know about the brand's products, its history, its styles, its design. Yet, if salespeople do not play their part well, if they are focused on chasing money rather than being brand ambassadors, this encounter can be counter-productive. The act of selling will have become heartless.

Salespeople are in a very important position, since they stand between the brand and the customer. Theirs is a tough profession, since they have to take on multiple roles:

- They are the drivers of the company.
- They see and sense the brand reality.
- They generate the money.
- They are on the front line, facing highly demanding customers.
- They are the first to observe changes.

- They are the missionaries of your brand philosophy.
- They observe the competition.
- They must multitask.
- They defend their brand.
- They are the first to identify problems.
- They are your brand's biggest media channel.
- They build your brand customer base.
- They must be able to distinguish between high and low customer potential.
- They make the brand human.
- They promote enthusiasm for the brand.
- They have to deal with diverse characters and cultures.
- They are like wine experts who hold hundreds of different flavors in their mind.
- They spread the brand message across the world.
- They are the storytellers for your brand.
- They can determine the brand's rise and fall.

> *I often defend the professions related to sales, since it is extremely hard to find a good salesperson. They are very interesting and rare people because they have to master a difficult task: mixing technicality with humanity.*
> (Natalie Bader, CEO of Prada France,
> former President at Fred International,
> former Marketing Director at Sephora)

Salespeople bring dynamism to your business. You can have the most beautiful brand on earth, the best store locations on earth, the best marketing on earth. But if you don't have a highly performing loyal sales force you are nothing. In economically difficult times especially, but also in general, I am convinced that salespeople are the most important people in your company. They are in front of the customer. They make the difference. Customers buy when they are satisfied, when they received advice from highly competent people who were, on top of that, friendly and sympathetic. Good salespeople are real brand ambassadors, who convey confidence in the brand. Despite this highly important and influential role, there are still so many companies that don't put the salesperson at the heart of their strategy. It is the same mistake as in a marriage: if you think that the wedding is the final and ultimate state of the relationship, you are totally wrong. The wedding is just the beginning of a long path that you need to walk together. The arrival of a salesperson within a company is just the same: it is the beginning of a, hopefully long, relationship between the salesperson and the brand. In order to allow sales advisors to represent the brand the best they can, all other departments and services around them should provide them with knowledge and expertise. They have to make them fit to fight in the battlefield.

Michel Guten, Sup de Luxe President,
Vice President Comité Champs-Élysées,
former Vice President of Cartier

With regard to recent changes in retail and brand environments, all the signs are pointing toward a steady increase in the importance of salespeople.

Contrary to what many might believe, the salesperson's role continues to expand considerably even as digital sales channels are emerging. The arrival of the Internet has provided brands with new ways of increasing their visibility, but, on the other hand, has also led to a constant "dehumanization." The Internet offers a virtual brand experience but takes away all human aspects. This is where boutiques can make the difference: in order to differentiate from the virtual world, physical stores must develop an even better human customer experience, with personal services provided by highly experienced, well-trained brand ambassadors who live and love their brand with great conviction. Why should I bother going out to a boutique if I can shop comfortably at home? The difference is this additional service, which is an unforgettable human experience (Figure 1). This is also what makes customers come back. It is similar to a restaurant: if your dish was fine but nothing special, but the service was exceptional due to a memorable atmosphere and warm human contact, you will probably return or recommend the place to your friends. In social media,

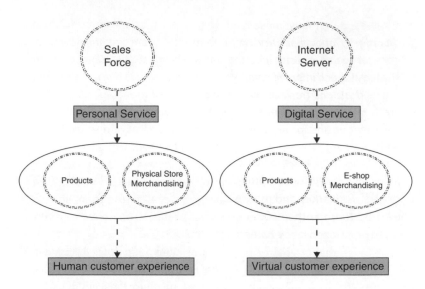

FIG 1 **Human versus virtual customer experience**

people talk about the service more than the product, since the product is what you expect to find anyway.

Besides, the Internet generates more and more demanding, highly informed customers. This requires salespeople to become the ultimate brand experts. When customers enter a brand boutique, they expect to have a real human experience, which can only be transmitted by such salespeople.

> *Studies show that customers tend to go online to discover the brand but then buy offline to experience the products. Therefore, I am convinced that the Internet obliges us to develop better professional and personal service in our stores, since this is the main difference between these two worlds.*

> (Natalie Bader, CEO of Prada France,
> former President at Fred International,
> former Director at Sephora)

The service provided by salespeople is the most distinctive element between luxury and mass-market retail environments. Yet many companies do not invest much effort or money in developing this.

Luxury brands have made huge progress with regard to product quality and innovation but they continue to neglect exceptional service, even though both aspects characterize a luxury product: quality and service. There is much improvement to be made: innovative ways of serving need to be lived and transmitted by salespeople.

(Christian Blanckaert, Professor in Luxury Management at ESCP Europe and former CEO of Hermès Sellier and Hermès International)

With intelligent mass-market brands such as Zara, H&M or UNIQLO becoming so powerful and providing good-quality products at the lowest price levels, it is more and more challenging for luxury brands to compete. They need to find other ways to remain distinctive and unique. One such way, as mentioned above, lies in providing highly exclusive, innovative service. This, again, requires members of your sales force to be closely linked to your brand, to defend it with passion and love from the bottom of their hearts, from morning till night.

If I push the reflection further I would even say that the product becomes the accessory of a pleasant moment, like the souvenir you bring home to remind you of a memorable trip. You want to keep this precious moment in your mind as long as possible.

(Alexandre Fauvet, former Executive Vice President at Lacoste)

This said, luxury shopping should be like a trip to your dreamworld. It is up to the salespeople to welcome their guests into this world, to help them feel comfortable and to stir up the customers' desire to bring back a nice souvenir from their trip to the luxury universe.

Even though it is obvious that the role of salespeople is crucial to the success of every brand and company, it is surprising how little considera-tion many brands used to or still give to this position within their organi-zation. Many top managers seem to be quite unaware of this problem and salespeople strongly feel it.

Unfortunately, there still are many companies that have not understood how important it is to focus on the well-being of those who are at the bottom of the boat. The latter are the ones who power the engine; they are rowing with all their strength to allow the luxury ferry to move ahead amidst all waves and storms. We, as salespeople, have such an important role to play, it is therefore unbelievable that we have been forsaken, since we are in the hold of the ship, making it move. The others are on the luxurious deck, several levels up. They don't go down the stairs to see or interact with us. We don't get the consideration we deserve even though we are the connection between the product and the customer. We are in the golden middle. You can compare it to a scale. If one side is too light, the scale drops on the other side. Why do I bring up this comparison? Well, if we don't get enough support from our brand management, we can't hold ourselves up in front of the customer. I very often feel that managers simply believe that their beautiful brands will sell even if all of their salespeople were gone.

(High-end jewelry sales manager)

In many companies, you can still find the traditional split between marketing and sales. This image of two separate worlds remains part of the business reality. On one side is the head office, including top management and all related services, and on the other side are the stores and salespeople out in the field. In my own professional experience, I experienced

ILL 1 / **Salespeople and management on a luxury ferry**

(Source: Albert Dessinateur for Michaela Merk)

the separation between these worlds many times; it is almost as if the inhabitants of both represented two enemy galaxies: the brand against the retail universe. In the luxury industry, this separation goes back to the traditional evolution of production and sales, as in the watch and jewelry business:

> *Originally, the watches were produced in workshops before being sent to sales companies, which were independent units. Production was not interested in sales and vice versa. Both universes represented two radically different professions and required skills that did not overlap at all. For that reason, we can still find brands, such as Rolex, which do not operate their own stores but focus exclusively on production and marketing. On a worldwide scale, local stores operate the point of sales for Rolex under a franchising distribution model.*
> (Arnaud Vidal, former Vice President Watches and Jewelry at Ralph Lauren and former General Manager of Audemars Piguet)

Even though both are governed by different rules and aspirations, I believe that the time has come to merge the brand and the retail worlds. The first signs that we are moving in this direction are the growing aspirations of brands to acquire retail experience. This is one of the reasons why the luxury empire LVMH acquired the selective perfumery chain Sephora, or why the beauty giant L'Oréal acquired the cosmetics retailer The Body Shop. When looking at a recent market study on retail evolutions in the luxury business, the trend that jumps out as obvious is that more and more luxury brands tend to expand their retail business faster than their wholesale business.[1]

Merging both worlds allows brands to better understand and learn from those in the field. Salespeople, on the other hand, could develop a better understanding of the difficulties of brand building and management. An ever-growing overlap between both worlds would lead to a stronger customer experience (Figure 2).

Unfortunately, as long as salespeople are not put at the heart of the company strategy, as long as they are not fully integrated within the global organization and as long as they continue to be seen as a less prestigious

---

[1] Bain & Company (2013) *Worldwide Luxury Market Monitor*, Spring.

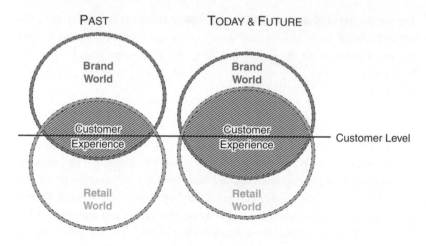

FIG 2 / **Brand world + retail world = customer experience**

entity, it will be hard for them to feel they are truly being treated with consideration and respect. It will also be difficult for them to develop close relationships with their corporation or brand.

Every brand and company should be conscious of the fact that salespeople, the "inhabitants" of the retail world, can no longer be regarded as inferior or less important. As long as they feel fully connected, integrated and respected, salespeople fulfill many crucial tasks that are essential to every brand's success.

This book aims to provide managers in the field of brand, retail, training, human resources and marketing with hands-on tools that will enable them to win the hearts of their sales staff. Winning salespeople's hearts means helping sales advisors develop strong relationships with the brands they represent. It also means developing strategies that will prevent vital salespeople from leaving a brand simply because a competitor offers a better salary. Instead of venturing into the vicious circle of constant payroll increase, this book develops alternative approaches for ensuring your sales teams remain attached to your brand.

In today's highly competitive markets, the real winners will be those who keep the rotation of the sales force at a very low level. In order to do so, a good relationship between the sales force and the brand is a must, not a choice.

Before providing 18 concrete heart-winning strategies, I want to highlight the emotional aspects that characterize strong and lasting relationships between salespeople and their brands. In the following chapter they will be illustrated through the image of the Olympic rings of sales force–brand relationships.

chapter 1

What Salespeople Feel in their Hearts: The Sales Force–Brand Relationship Olympic Rings

Using the qualitative and quantitative research of my PhD studies, I have been able to clearly identify relationship patterns between salespeople and their brands – patterns similar to the interpersonal relationship characteristics that occur when two people like or love each other. Before we look at the facets of these relationships let us see how research defines this widely used term. The British psychologist and ethnologist Robert A. Hinde puts forward four central conditions that allow us to talk about a relationship:[1]

1. When both partners actively and independently exchange with each other.
2. When both partners decide to engage while being driven by mutual aims.
3. When the relationship allows both partners to benefit from each other.
4. When the commitment's dynamic slightly changes and evolves over time.

It could be said that it is impossible to interact with brands since they are just simple objects. How can someone actively enter into a relationship with an object, a logo or a product? This argument is exactly why it is

---

[1] Robert A. Hinde (1979) *Towards Understanding Relationships*. London: Academy Press.

so important to bring our brands to life, to breathe a soul in them, to make them human. This phenomenon has been studied by J. Aaker,[2] and goes back to the first theories of animism that suggest we have a permanent need to anthropomorphize objects so that interactions with the nonmaterial world can be facilitated.[3] The personification of brands can be achieved by associating brands with spokespeople such as famous movie stars and by reinforcing the role of the brand's creator, its representatives or the general manager.

While the relationship between salespeople and their brands has been completely underresearched, scholars have shared interesting insights on the relationship patterns between customers and brands. They have examined why customers remained extremely loyal to certain brands, why they dressed from head to toe in only one brand, why they kept talking about it or why they dreamt about it. Susan Fournier has been among the first to develop a model that includes six dimensions characterizing these consumer–brand relationships:[4]

1. Love and passion for the brand.
2. Identification (or self-connection) with the brand.
3. Brand partner quality expressed through feelings of trust and reliability.
4. Brand commitment as a commitment in the long run.
5. Interdependence resulting from frequent brand use.
6. Intimacy deriving from personal experiences with the brand.

Working from these findings, I wanted to get a better understanding of the relationships I had observed throughout my professional career and that I consider crucial for every brand's success: the sales force–brand relationships. I wanted to know what salespeople felt inside their hearts when relationships were strong, and which emotional facets characterized these relationships compared with consumer–brand relationships.

---

[2] J. Aaker (1997) "Dimensions of brand personality," *Journal of Marketing Research*, 34 (August), 347–57.
[3] G. W. Gilmore (1919) *Animism*. Boston: Marshall Jones. W. McDougall (1911) *Body and Mind: A History and Defense of Animism*. New York: Macmillan.
[4] S. Fournier (1998) "Consumers and their brands: developing relationship theory in consumer research." *Journal of Consumer Research*, 24, 343–73.

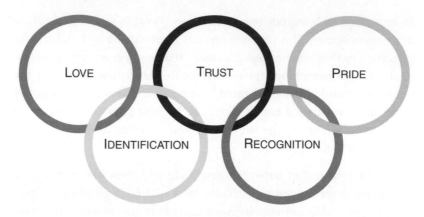

FIG 3 / The sales force–brand relationship Olympic rings

By analyzing the hundreds of interviews conducted in field research I was able to distinguish five dimensions which form the "Five Olympic Rings of Sales Force–Brand Relationships" (Figure 3):

1. Love and passion for the brand.
2. Identification with the brand.
3. Trust in the brand.
4. The pride of belonging to the brand.
5. Recognition for brand expertise.

While love, identification and trust are emotions shared by consumers and salespeople when forming strong relationships with brands, pride and recognition occur exclusively in a sales context.

When brands succeed in stimulating all five relationship dimensions, they lay the best foundation by turning their sales associates into brand champions. These brand champions are brand ambassadors who burn for their brand. They carry the flame of victory and can lead their brand to tremendous success.

Let's look more closely at these five emotional aspects in order to understand what salespeople feel in their hearts when the flame is burning.

1.1   LOVE is in the air

We all know this amazing feeling that fills your entire body, and makes your stomach tingle. Feelings of love have an incredible power on our inner energy and the energy we transmit to others. Feelings of love are something supernatural and intangible.

When we are in love, we behave differently; we do things more intensely, with a smile on our faces. Scholars define love as part of an affective state that occurs at various levels of intensity, from liking, loving, feelings of passion and even addiction. All these states of affection were present in one form or another when I interviewed salespeople who strongly related to their brand. Here are some passionate representative statements:

"What motivates me every day is the strong emotion I feel for my brand. This feeling lies deep inside my heart."

(Lancôme sales representative)

"In order to sell, we need to love what we sell. Otherwise it does not work. This is inevitable."

(Longchamp store manager)

"When I suggest a brand I love to a client, I speak about it easily with passion, I provide more information and suggest it more often."

(Sephora sales advisor)

"The arrival of a new product is like a baby born in a family. It's always an exciting moment."

(Store manager, high-end watchmaking)

"The Sephora brand is my baby. I got to know the brand very well over the years, I grew up with it in the company and I now defend it like a mother defends her child. I really fell in love with the brand."

(Sephora sales advisor)

"I like the feeling of being closely related to my brand. This stimulates my working energy every day."

(Fendi sales associate)

> *"I need to have a strong emotional connection with my brand, otherwise I couldn't enjoy selling it and the days would be incredibly long."*
>
> (Fendi sales manager)
>
> *"When you like selling you can sell a bit of everything. But you need to be passionate about your brand in order to experience the entire dimension of your brand. Your degree of implication is much higher when you love your brand and its products."*
>
> (Cartier store manager)
>
> *"If you are not passionate about your brand, it is incredibly hard to start the selling ritual again and again. You need to enjoy explaining, demonstrating and repeating the same information over and over again to your customers. You really sell with your heart. If you don't sell with your heart, it gets complicated."*
>
> (High-end watchmaking store manager)
>
> *"I never thought that the intensity of loving my brand had such an impact on my sales performance. Without love, no pleasure."*
>
> (Fred sales advisor)

These statements clearly show what salespeople believe: without passion there is no pleasure, no success.

The love and affection we feel for good friends is not very different from the feelings salespeople develop for the brands they sell. Love is there, as long as the good sides of products prevail.

> *If you want to have friends and love, only look at their positive sides; if you begin looking at their negative sides, there will no longer be friends and love.*
>
> *For products, it's exactly the same thing: We are aware of their bad sides in order to show that those are secondary to the good ones.*
>
> Michel Guten, Sup de Luxe President,
> Vice President Comité Champs Elysées, former Vice President of Cartier

In contrast, managers tend to be skeptical about salespeople expressing too much passion for their brand. They prefer salespeople to be experts instead of being fans. Managers think that salespeople should enhance their clients' passion instead of rival with them. If salespeople are too passionate about their brand or the activity related to it, they are on equal terms with the customer and roles are blurred.

> *Salespeople who are too passionate don't listen to their customers since they talk too much about themselves. They destroy the customers' pride by making them feel inferior. Salespeople should be excellent technicians, not passionate. For instance, I love playing tennis. When I enter a tennis shop and the salesperson tells me that he is an excellent tennis player I feel uncomfortable, as if my opinion no longer counted, as if I had to accept his advice.*
> (Arnaud Vidal, former Vice President Watches and Jewelry at Ralph Lauren and former General Manager of Audemars Piguet)

It is important that salespeople always respect their customers' passion first, instead of simply demonstrating their own passion.

How can we see that love is in the air?

There are a number of indicators that allow you to detect when your sales associates have fallen in love with the brand they represent:

1 – A desire to touch

Salespeople who love their brand feel a strong desire to be close to their products. They admire them, touch them, caress them, smell them. All their senses interact with the brand. In fashion, this becomes obvious when salespeople caress the fabric of the shirt, the coat or the pair of trousers that they are presenting to their customer. In cosmetics, salespeople who love their brand are impatient to test all kinds of textures at home. They want to experience their brand and be as close to it as possible.

2 – An explosion of creativity

Salespeople who are in love with their brand develop a remarkable sense of aesthetics and become very creative. They immediately know which products to combine and are very successful at cross-selling products, which is a very important skill in sales in order to increase the average purchase basket.

Similarly, when it comes to merchandising, brand-loving salespeople intuitively display products and are always concerned about highlighting the best in their beloved brand.

3 – Natural spontaneity

Salespeople serve many customers over the course of a day. Every customer and case is different and requires the salesperson to adapt in order to successfully master the new sales scenario.

The more salespeople love their brand, the easier it will be for them to find the most fitting and convincing words when interacting with the customer, even with the extremely demanding ones. All sale arguments should become very natural, spontaneous and honest.

> *Luxury customers are very demanding and most of them are filled with passion, especially in the watches and jewelry sector. They want to know what kind of salesperson is advising them. They test your level of expertise. But I enjoy being tested, since high-end watches are my passion. I talk naturally about anything the customer wants to know in this field. And if anyone wants to test my knowledge they are most welcome. At the same time we also test the customers' expertise just to establish a balanced level of discussion.*
>
> (Assistant store manager and after sales services manager at a
> high-end watchmaking brand)

4 – A passion to transmit

Brand-loving salespeople feel an immense desire to pass on the message, the stories, the secrets, the expertise and all they know about their beloved brand to those around them: to friends, family members and especially to their customers. They want everyone to know for which brand they burn and fight for each day and how much they know about it. The way they transmit information is often poetic, with beautifully chosen words.

> *Every morning I can't wait to go to my boutique. I need to feel close to my brand, to my customers and I feel this strong desire to transmit. Today I apply everything I've learned in my previous working experiences. I transmit my passion, tell the customers stories, I try to give them the brand's general culture. In luxury it is important to transmit a general knowledge. I also transmit everything I've learned from the customers themselves, even very famous ones such as Lady Diana, for example.*
>
> (Store manager at a high-end watchmaking brand)

I'm thinking of a salesperson who had been working for St Laurent for 15 years. He could explain every single detail of the collections to his customers: when the garments had been created, Mr St Laurent's inspirations or which new materials he used to design his masterpieces. He was burning for the brand, its techniques and the creator. His words were magic. He built such strong ties with his customers because he managed to fascinate them all.

(Jean-Charles Champey, former Store Manager at Yves Saint Laurent)

5 – Giving human features to objects

When salespeople feel passionate about their brand and its products, they create such a strong relationship that they talk about the products as if they were human beings. Objects take on human traits: they can talk, smell and hear. This emerges because such a strong connection has been established between the object and the person.

You can't even find the adequate words to describe the endless pleasure a precious stone can bring. These materials speak and you need to understand them, detect what they say and translate their words. However, you should never divulge everything, never disclose all the secrets. I learned to listen to the stones by reading a lot and hearing what they had to say from within their gut. You need to understand what is going on from the inside.

(Paul Bassène, High Jewelry Manager at Cartier)

6 – Endless effort

Salespeople who are filled with passion and love for their brand would do anything for it, even without being asked to do so. Nothing is too much, effort is above expectations and working time is timeless.

1.2   IDENTIFICATION:
My brand, my customer and I

A certain degree of brand identification is required in order to establish strong relationships between the brand and salespeople.

The notion of brand identification derives from the social identity theory which asserts that people strive for psychological membership in various social groups.[5] In addition, people use objects to remind themselves of who they are and to indicate who they are to others.[6] In some cases, strong personal self-identification with a brand can lead to feelings of protection and dependency.[7]

Thanks to the hundreds of interviews I have held, I have been able to detect five criteria that lead to salespeople strongly identifying with the brands they were recommending and selling (see Figure 4).

FIG 4 / The sales force–brand identification cycle

---

[5] H. Tajfel (1978) "The achievement of group differentiation." In: H. Tajfel, *Differentiation between Social Groups: Studies in the Social Psychology of Intergroup Relations.* London: Academic Press, 77–98.

[6] M. Wallendorf and E. Arnould (1989) "My favorite things: a cross-cultural inquiry into object attachment, possessiveness, and social linkage." *Journal of Consumer Research*, 14, 531–47.

[7] S. M. Drigotas and C. E. Rusbult (1992) "Should I stay or should I go? A dependence model of breakups." *Journal of Personality and Social Psychology*, 62 (January), 62–87.

Which factors lead to strong identification between the sales force and their brand?

The "sales force–brand identification cycle" shows the five facets that foster brand identification.

1 – Admiration

Admiration creates desire and lets you dream. A world of fascination surrounds brands, especially luxury brands.

> *Cartier has always been a brand that fascinated me. There is such an extraordinary aura around this brand, everything is shining, beautiful, aesthetic. All is love for endless detail. I felt admiration on the very first day when I stepped into a boutique for my job interview.*
>
> (Cartier store manager)

2 – Passion

Many strong luxury brands have been created out of passion and are linked to activities that go far beyond the products themselves. Lacoste was created out of a passion for tennis, Hermès out of a fascination for horses. Louis Vuitton loves sailing, Rolex loves golf and Ralph Lauren, polo. If salespeople share this same passion, the identification process is almost guaranteed. A sales associate working at Repetto, a brand created out of passion for ballet dancing, explained:

> *Repetto is my story. Even when I sell a bag I talk about dancing. There is a bag called 'Cabriole.' In my sales ritual I always demonstrate the cabriole, which is a ballet movement. Obviously, at that moment, my customers are so surprised that they are taken away from reality into a dream. Whenever I get back from the storage area to the boutique, I feel like I'm going on-stage again. To me, selling is like a theater with an ever-changing audience. And you, the salesperson, are the main-actor interacting with your audience. The more you can transmit your passion, the more your audience will play with you, will identify with your brand and buy no matter what the price is.*
>
> (Sales associate at Repetto)

> *I consider the boutique to be a theater full of relationships. In the morning I arrive on my motorbike wearing jeans. Then, I change clothes and jump*

ILL 2 / **Salesperson on stage**

(Source: Albert Dessinateur for Michaela Merk)

> *into my role like an actor on stage, and open the curtain. In order to smile,*
> *you need to leave all your problems at home. We can replace each other*
> *when someone is sick, like in a theater group. This is true team spirit.*
> (Store manager at a high-end watchmaking brand)

3 – Culture

Brand identification thrives on cultural assimilation. Salespeople who share the same nationality as their brand's origin unite more easily with their brand. This can be explained because of certain feelings of pride and nostalgia but also because of an understanding of the culture: everything is familiar, homely. His/her brand is therefore no stranger but rather a compatriot or even a family member.

> *When working for an Italian brand as an Italian, everything feels like*
> *home: the sophistication, the Roman glamour, the Italian charm.*
> (Store manager at Miu Miu)

4 – Age

Sales associates and representatives who are at the heart of the brand's target group identify more easily with its philosophy, products, values and style. When in discussion with Sephora sales advisors it became clear that the younger members of the sales force easily identified with these young and fresh brands. They felt comfortable with these brands and had fun selling them to a younger target group since they naturally represented their own lifestyle and mindset.

5 – Character assimilation

Salespeople's assimilation to a brand's values, style and character is at the heart of the identification process. The closer the values are aligned, the more a salesperson feels comfortable, and selling therefore becomes natural.

> *I can fully identify with the brand Herborist because I believe in its philosophy. Being built on the principles of Chinese healing arts, the brand succeeded in transforming nature's concept of Yin and Yang into its products. I do believe that beauty comes from the inside as well as the outside and for this reason the balance of body and soul is essential. This is how I live and this is what makes me truly live my brand every day in sales and in my trainings for Douglas.*
>
> (Maicen Neu, Brand Representative and Trainer at Herborist)

An Agent Provocateur store manager explained during our interview that she immediately felt good when she started working for her brand since it was a beautiful, sexy and audacious brand, which corresponded to her character. This helped her become very successful in her job. When she talked about the products, customers believed her because everything seemed authentic.

How can we see that salespeople identify with the brand they sell?

The most obvious sign of visible identification is when salespeople use or wear the brand outside of their working environment; when the brand enters the private sphere.

> *When I saw that salespeople were wearing Lacoste shirts in their private lives, I knew that Lacoste was about to win their hearts. By doing this,*

they pursue the sales ritual simply by wearing the brand. All brands should reach this point.

(Alexandre Fauvet, former Executive Vice President at Lacoste)

We also notice that brand identification leads to stronger assimilation over time: salespeople begin to speak in the words of their brand, they begin to like its style and behave accordingly. If the brand were to change, the salespeople would also gradually change.

Is brand identification always good?

Although salespeople feel that identifying with their brand is essential to establish a close relationship with it, managers also highlight two dangers related to the identification process:

1 – The danger of the salesperson assimilating with the brand creator

The biggest risk linked to strong brand identification takes place when salespeople talk about their brand as if they had created it themselves, as if they were behind the products' genius ideas and the brand's entire philosophy. When this happens, salespeople no longer behave as salespeople but as the brand owner, which is damaging for the brand and unpleasant for the customers.

> *There are examples of stores where customers feel as if they are entering into the store manager's boutique when they should feel welcome to enter the brand's home, not the salesperson's home. The customer should be treated like a king, but if store managers identify too much with their brand, they are the ones pretending to be the kings and behaving as if they were Louis Cartier in person.*
>
> *(Nathalie Banessy Monasterio,*
> *former Retail Development Director at Richemont)*

One of the biggest dangers in the world of luxury is that the big brands carry such tremendous status for those who champion them, that most people can't resist the temptation of total identification. Human nature is so weak that many are willing to give up their own authentic personality, begin feeling like superstars, creating virtual creatures around them. They believe in incarnating the brand themselves. Curiously enough, once they leave the brand, they become normal again, no matter the level – be it the General Manager or his driver. While they become normal again, the brand persists. You need to understand that the brand is something that's almost sacred, much stronger than manhood. Therefore you need to be humble to serve the brand and you must love it to help it grow into a beautiful tree some day. You should never confuse the brand with yourself. Simplicity and respectfulness towards your brand should be translated in your daily interactions with people in your company. This begins by greeting everyone and talking to them in a normal, respectful way.

Alain Dominique Perrin, Non-Executive Director at Richemont Group,
former President of Cartier International,
President of EFMD (European Foundation for Management Development)
and President of EDC (École des Dirigeants et Créateurs d'Entreprises)

2 – The danger of the salesperson assimilating with the customer

If salespeople identify too strongly with their brand, they develop a strong desire to purchase the products for themselves. When this happens, roles change and salespeople become customers. However, customers don't want to purchase from another customer but from a highly professional brand expert who is advising them in the most qualified way. Nathalie Banessy Monasterio underlines the fact that most customers are not receptive to sale arguments such as *"Take this product, it's great. I bought the same one for myself."* These types of situations occur when salespeople identify with the brand without being properly trained.

The role of salespeople is not an easy one. Finding the right balance between professionalism and brand identification is like walking on a tightrope (Illustration 3). The challenge lies in staying out of the customer's sphere but remaining a knowledgeable, inspiring and serviceable mediator between the brand and the customer.

ILL 3 / **Walking the customer–brand tightrope**

(Source: Albert Dessinateur for Michaela Merk)

A highly successful sales manager at Cartier shared reflections with me about the dangers of salespeople putting themselves on the same level as customers:

> *Even though I am highly successful in my profession, I would not buy a luxury villa next to my customer. I would rather hide, since the customer should never know that I have been successful. I am his confidant and probably know more of his secrets than his own wife. But I need to keep these secrets to myself until my death, like a priest, which is a huge responsibility. You need to remain extremely humble, serve your client at every moment, listen to him but never put yourself at the same level. Otherwise you break the mystery of your brand which is the strongest asset it has.*

1.3   TRUST: I can count on you!

Like love, trust is a key emotional dimension in every relationship. Without trust, no relationship can last. Scientists who studied this element in depth found that trust was essential to all relational exchanges.[8] It can be associated with honesty, fairness, consistency, competence, responsibility, confidence and integrity.[9] They also found that trust had to be earned and could not be obtained on demand.[10] Brands must therefore establish a personal link with each salesperson in order to build a certain degree of intimacy.

When salespeople do not trust their brand and its products, they cannot cope with their profession and end up leaving their jobs. A fashion brand sales associate told me:

> *If I sell a product which I don't believe in myself, I don't consider it to be a successful sale. I feel sad, bad and empty at the end of the day. We could all lie to our customers, but in the long run we couldn't take it and would quit.*

The benefits of a trusting sales force

1 – No fear when recommending

Salespeople who trust their brand are those who dare to sell. They are prepared to argue for their products, to counter objections, to confront any possible sales situation. They are as fit as sportsmen keen on entering a competition, since they know that they have acquired all the necessary skills to win.

2 – No fear about price

In luxury, where prices are high, trust is even more important. Without the full trust of your sales force, highly priced products don't sell. How is it possible to be convincing when you are not convinced yourself? It's only when trust is fully established that the price no longer becomes an issue.

---

[8] R. M. Morgan and S. D. Hunt (1994) "The commitment-trust theory of relationship marketing." *Journal of Marketing*, 58, 20–38.
[9] C. Moorman, R. Deshpadé and G. Zaltman (1993) "Factors affecting trust in market research relationships." *Journal of Marketing*, 57 (January), 81–101.
[10] M. Blackston (1992) "Observations: building brand equity by managing the brand's relationships." *Journal of Advertising Research* (May/June), 79–83.

Your teams can then purely focus on their sales ritual. The immediate impact on your brand's turnover is guaranteed!

The two spheres in the trust-building process

During my interviews, I was able to identify two general orientations in the trust-building process for salespeople (see Figure 5).

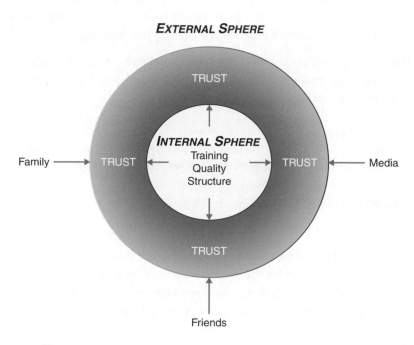

FIG 5 The two spheres in the trust-building process

1 – Trust from outside the brand

Some salespeople trust the brand even before they start selling it. This is especially true for luxury brands, where family members and friends can have a huge impact on the quality of the relationship a salesperson has with a certain brand. Heritage is a main vector of trust. When parents give a TAG Heuer watch to their son, they instantaneously transmit their trust in this brand to him. When you receive from your closest family members your first Hermès scarf or a Tiffany necklace for your 30th birthday, you begin to establish a trusting relationship with the brand from that moment on. When your best friend drives a Porsche and keeps talking about its excellent reliability on the road, your trust is gained, too.

Beyond the social influence, media also increases trust in brands at an early stage. Any kind of above-the-line communication – from advertising on TV, to the press, to the Internet or events – contribute in conveying trust, even before the salesperson joins the company.

2 – Trust from within the brand

There are several ways to help salespeople trust their brand once they have joined the ranks of the company: regular internal information sessions, early-stage brand training sessions, high product quality, a trustworthy CEO and good organizational structures. We will focus on these aspects in depth in Chapter 2.

Brands that don't lose sight of their key expertise have a better chance of gaining their salespeople's trust than brands that are constantly diversifying. Trust, for instance, is particularly strong among salespeople who work for the core expertise within a brand. The brand's savoir faire is reflected in its expertise, such as fur for Fendi, haute couture for Dior or leather for Hermès. This brand expertise forms the base and credibility of each brand, which salespeople need to be able to trust. Based upon this trust they are then able to transmit the essence of the brand to their customers.

Some salespeople gain trust in their brand because the corporation trusted them at a certain stage in their career.

> *Within less than a year they gave me the opportunity to manage a store, even though I had never done this before. This gave me confidence and I started trusting the brand, which fostered my relationship with it.*
>
> (Yves Saint Laurent store manager)

Mutual trust is then established between salespeople and their employer.

> *During the twelve years that I was working for Montblanc, I created strong ties with the brand and with my colleagues. This is due to the brand's trust in me and allowed me to progress. I became something like a reference within the company and I had many big customers. Whenever there was a problem, they called me first. Whenever a new manager*

*arrived, he was trained at my point of sale. It was extremely hard for me
to leave this brand.*

(Former store manager at Montblanc)

1.4 PRIDE: We are the best!

Another emotional component that tightens salespeople's relationships
with their brand is their feeling of pride.

One of the first scientists to study pride was Darwin.[11] He suggests that
"of all the complex emotions, pride, perhaps, is the most plainly expressed.
It is the only self-conscious emotion that has a reliably recognized, universal expression throughout all cultures." At the age of four, children are
supposed to be able to make out the nonverbal expression for pride.[12] The
psychologists J. L. Tracy and R. W. Robins distinguish two different kinds
of pride:[13] authentic pride and hubristic pride. The former is related to pro-
social, achievement-oriented conceptualization deriving from accomplishments and confidence. In this sense, the positive feelings of belonging to a
high-status group reflect a sign of pride. Hubristic pride, however, fits with
self-aggrandizement, arrogance and narcissism. Scientists have found that
pride served both survival and social functions. After a successful action
or achievement, an individual feels a sense of pride, which might lead to
higher self-esteem over time. In addition, proud people tend to show a
strong desire to contact others and inform them of their own success.

From my studies, I have been able to distinguish two different types of
pride experienced by salespeople in relation to the brand they were selling:

1 – Pride of belonging

Salespeople feel extremely proud of working for a brand that projects
beyond their stores, that is famous, has a great reputation, represents

---

[11] C. Darwin ([1872] 1998) *The Expression of the Emotions in Man and Animals* (3rd
edn.). New York: Oxford University Press.

[12] D. Stipek, S. Recchia and S. McClintic (1992) "Self-evaluation in young Children."
Monographs of the Society for Research in Child Development, 57(1) (serial no. 226).

[13] J. L. Tracy and R. W. Robins (2004) "Show your pride: evidence for a discrete emotion
expression." *Psychological Science*, 15, 194–7.

ultimate luxury, incorporates strong values and a unique identity. A Louis Vuitton sales assistant confirmed that they were primarily not working for salary, but for the brand. They were all proud of belonging to this magic brand of international fame. They lived for Vuitton.

Salespeople consider being part of this brand an immense privilege, which allows them to discover collections, advertising campaigns, merchandising designs and anything new around the brand before the customer and even the press. It makes them feel like VIPs. When salespeople work for a brand for a long period of time, their pride of belonging strengthens, especially when they get to know the brand creator or the founder him- or herself.

2 – Pride due to success

Another form of pride exists in relation to success. Market leadership, for instance, generates pride.

> *I am so proud of Lancôme for being one of the leading cosmetics brands worldwide thanks to all the efforts that were previously put into the brand. I am eager to push the brand forward even further.*
>
> (Sandrine Sabathé, Sales Representative at Lancôme)

Salespeople who succeed within their brands feel extremely proud when they achieve important sales progressions, when they increase their customer portfolio or when they sell expensive products to their customers.

> *Our team felt so proud about achieving the highest progression rate of all Fendi stores last year. I personally feel extremely proud when I manage to sell a bag not only to one person but to an entire group of friends. Especially when they mention having seen bags at other brands, gone there, and came back again to purchase mine.*
>
> (Fendi store manager)

Pride linked to success can also happen when the brand breeds talent, when salespeople become future managers. Salespeople feel proud of working for a brand that has great career potential, not only for themselves but also for others, especially their own team members. A Chanel store manager told me how proud she felt when her colleagues and

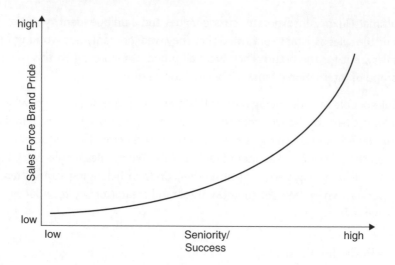

FIG 6 / The curve of salespeople's pride

subordinates went in many different directions and always kept positive memories of their brand.

"The curve of salespeople's pride" shows that pride is not static but evolves over time and intensity (Figure 6).

1.5   RECOGNITION: Because I'm worth it!

The next brand-relationship component is recognition. Recognition is a very complex phenomenon in our society. Recognition and respect are fundamental to any long-lasting interpersonal relationship. It is only when there is mutual respect that a relationship can remain harmonious.

Scientists who examined recognition agreed that all individuals, both in a social and working context, need recognition regardless of their status or their profession.[14] It can be defined as a judgment made about a person's contribution, personal dedication, engagement and performance.

---

[14] J. P. Brun and N. Dugas (2008) "An analysis of employee recognition: perspectives on human resources practices." *The International Journal of Human Resource Management*, 19(4), 716–30.

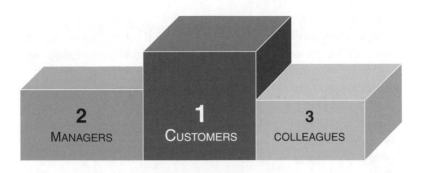

FIG 7 / The three pillars of sales force recognition

Recognition helps individuals preserve and build their identity but also their well-being, both in a personal and professional context.

It is interesting to examine what kind of recognition salespeople expect to meet.

I have been able to identify three types of recognition, which I call the "Three pillars of sales force recognition".

1. Recognition expressed by customers.
2. Recognition expressed by sales management.
3. Recognition expressed by colleagues.

Of the three pillars, customers have the strongest influence on salespeople's feelings of recognition. This has been confirmed by all those interviewed.

Alexandre Ferragu, former Retail Sales Manager Luxury and Accessories at Printemps, underlines this:

> *The recognition salespeople get from customers for their expertise is even more important than recognition by their sales managers. This is especially true in a department store like ours, where thousands of customers enter every day. Some of them even*

come back to see their sales advisor several times a week. While we offer more or less the same brands as our neighbor Galeries Lafayette, it is the interaction between the salesperson and the customer that makes the difference. Customers come back if they are satisfied with the service provided due to exceptional expertise. This is the kind of recognition salespeople live for. We have salespeople who have been here for over 30 years. It is neither the salary that keeps them going, nor recognition from their managers who rarely remain for a long time in the store. No, what keeps them going are their customers who respect them for their brand expertise and who keep coming back over the years.

Why do customers recognize their salesperson?

1 – For irreproachable service

Customers who are satisfied because of excellent service will usually thank you in words. Some customers, like the Chinese, don't express their recognition for service in words but by the fact that they come back and bring their friends along.

(Sales associate at Longchamp)

2 – For professionalism

Customers express recognition when salespeople are professional and offer excellent service: when they know their stock level, when their desired products are made available, when they can explain the specificities of the product and can provide any kind of advice related to their brand.

A store manager at a high-end lingerie brand mentioned that the best compliment a customer can make her is to say *"you are so professional."*

3 – For honesty

A store manager at a luxury leather goods store told me that sometimes customers came back to her months after their purchase in order to thank her for her honest advice in selling a pair of high-quality shoes that were suitable for any situation.

4 – For sympathy

When you serve your customers with a smile on your face and interact with them filled with passion, they will come back to see only you. What could be more fulfilling?

(Repetto sales associate)

What salespeople love about customer recognition is that the task of selling goes beyond the realm of a simple transaction and acquires a human touch.

Some customers are so grateful when they get good service that they come back to bring us chocolate or candles. Other customers just come to say 'hello' or they bring along their kids. This is wonderful and really important to me.

(Fendi store manager)

The following chapter will provide managers with concrete, heart-winning tools that allow managers:

– to bind salespeople closer to their brands
– to enhance team spirit
– to increase customer satisfaction
– to stimulate sales force motivation
– to strengthen loyalty to your company and brand.

2

Luxury Relationship Branding: Heart-Winning Strategies for Brand Managers and their Corporations

Using the five emotional facets that characterize the relationships sales-people have with their brands, in this chapter I provide 18 heart-winning strategies. Together they form the Luxury Relationship Branding – Strategies. Putting these in place, managers can bind the sales force even more closely to brands and corporations without necessarily getting into the vicious cycle of paying more and more money to make people stay.

There are other, more effective management tools that are much more closely related to human behavior than to money. The results of the interviews I conducted clearly showed that emotions formed bonds that lasted longer than money. The following chapter will show you how to implement emotional management in order to maximize the relationship between the sales force and the brand, stimulate salespeople's motivation and create strong salesperson brand loyalty.

2.1   How to ignite salespeople's love

Heart-winner 1: Fill your brand with heart and soul!

Relationships with brands can only emerge when they are brought to life and filled with personality and human traits: in sum, when you give your brand a heart and a soul.

Most brands already have a soul: their creator's. It just needs to be highlighted to make it visible to the outside world; only then can salespeople and their customers develop strong feelings for the brand.

Some brand creators become icons such as Coco Chanel and Yves Saint Laurent. Others have remained confidential. Alain Nemarq, President of Mauboussin, refers to his collaboration with Yves Saint Laurent with nostalgia:

> *These creators are geniuses. I always call them wizards, since they have something extraterrestrial, exceptional, unreachable, a sense of overflowing creativity. They are the heart and soul of a brand. It's only if a brand is able to keep this precious and unique soul that employees, and especially salespeople, can stay enflamed for it.*

With such a strong foundation, the basement, walls and roof of a company's "house" or "castle" – depending on the brand's greatness – can be built. Employees and salespeople can decorate the house and give it its style: sometimes rather classical, sometimes rebellious, colorful, natural or simply crazy.

Preserving the brand's essence and origin is a huge asset in the relationship-building process between brands and salespeople. This human aspect makes brands tangible, brings them to life and gives them heart and soul. Brands become personalities to admire and to love.

In the era of storytelling, every brand must elaborate the story of its origins:

- Who created it?
- What was the creator's personality?
- What inspired him/her during the creation process?
- What motivated him/her?
- What are his/her values and beliefs?
- What was his/her particular talent?
- What did s/he create first?
- What were the obstacles in the creation process?
- What unexpected moments occurred during the creation?
- When did the breakthrough take place?

- Who bought the products first?
- What heralded success?

In the hundreds of interviews I held with salespeople working for premium and luxury brands I realized how important it is to highlight the role of the brand creator.

Giving the brand a soul:

- brings it to life
- makes it tangible, lovable
- makes it credible, real
- reflects its excellence
- generates admiration
- facilitates identification
- makes it desirable
- provides stories.

The more details salespeople gave me about their creators, the more I could feel that the fire was burning. Let me share some of the stories I was told:

> *Fendi has an amazing history and it is one of the rare brands where some-one from the family still works for the brand. Silvia Fendi, the founder's great-granddaughter, is our artistic director. Whatever is being designed goes through her hands. Thus, all products that are delivered to our stores make more sense since the family is still involved.*
>
> (Fendi store manager)

> *Madame Repetto was the mother of Roland Petit, a great ballet dancer at the Paris Opera House. She started sewing ballet shoes for her son and the other dancers loved these. So she started producing shoes for all ballet dancers at the Opera Garnier. In 1956, Brigitte Bardot, who was a dancer before she entered the movie world, asked Madame Repetto to make her a pair of very flexible shoes in order to be able to dance in the movie Et Dieu créa la femme (And God Created Woman). Bardot often linked her success back to those shoes. Even as a salesperson, I was lucky enough to get to know Madame Repetto myself when she was still working in her boutique. She was so charismatic and had incredible connections with the*

worlds of film and theater. Even though she died in the 1980s, her spirit remains in all of our shoes.

(Repetto sales associate)

Fred Samuel, the founder of the luxury brand Fred used to live in Argentina. He left France during the Second World War to be closer to the sun and to follow his passions for traveling and sailing. According to the stories I've heard about him and his life, he had a strong personality that was filled with sunshine, generosity and joy just as his sons and his wife did. He was a smiling, truly sympathetic and dynamic person. Today, his spirit still impacts on the entire brand and its salespeople.

(Fred sales associate)

Stories about brand creators who have passed away are often told with nostalgia, almost like a fairytale. Stories about living brand creators are emotional due to their personal proximity and talent. I could sense in the people I interviewed a certain pride if they knew and served the brand's original creators. This proximity is even stronger in family-owned businesses, as is the case for Patrick Roger, the famous artistic luxury chocolate designer:

We are a family business. Everyone admires and loves the chef for his extraordinary character and talent. He is more than just a chocolate producer; he is a sculptor and an artist. You need to enter into the world of Patrick Roger in order to understand him as a person. Then you will love what you sell and talk about love when selling his chocolate.

(Corinne Roger, Retail and Human Resources Director at Patrick Roger)

However, brands can also tell heart-winning stories without necessarily referring to their creator. What is important is to create an incredible mystery around your brand and its products. Such stories must be filled with characters of exceptional talent, with poetry, beauty, magic and emotion. They should help customers and salespeople dive into a dream-world – for customers when they listen to the stories and for salespeople when they tell them.

Our world is full of fairies, magnificent butterflies, flowers. In the world in which we live especially, people need something to dream about. Therefore we innovate to help people dream and escape from everyday

life. Look at my finger ring. It is called Socrate, one of our best-selling
rings. When you wear it, you have the impression of wearing four flowers
between your fingers. There is a story related to each piece of art.

(Brigitte Smadja, Store Manager at Van Cleef & Arpels)

You can generate mystery around your products by referring to the use of precious, rare materials that are mother earth's gift to us. In high-end jewelry, these are the unique stones that go back thousands of years in evolution:

All these magic gems go back more than 2000 years. We don't even quite
know how they emerged. We need to pay our highest respect to those
stones that have magic powers: the opal protects us, the diamond offers
blessings, the rubies make us powerful, and others offer us calming rays.
They are nature's creations, deriving from our earth's genesis.

(Paul Bassène, High Jewelry Manager at Cartier)

These stories were told with so much enthusiasm that I could see how important it is for a brand to have depth and transmit this in an authentic and poetic way. Customers love stories, and salespeople love them too. If salespeople can pass on stories that are filled with heart and soul, you have managed to achieve the first "heart-winner" among your sales force.

Creating these stories alone is not sufficient. You need to reflect on how you pass on the flame to others, within and outside your brand organization.

That's what I believe: let them feel the heartbeat of your brand and they will fall in love with it.

Heart-winner 2: Pass on the flame!

The brand creator's aura is a real treasure that must be preserved and passed on through generations. The creator's message is the heart of the brand and it needs to have a sacred dimension. *"Your sales force will be strong as long as it gets the impression of preaching a holy message to the world."* (Alain Nemarq, President of Mauboussin). So what can brands do in order to facilitate the transmission process? How can we make sure that the flame of passion for the brand will never stop burning even though many people will hold it in their hands and pass it on?

ILL 4 / Passing over the flame

(Source: Albert Dessinateur for Michaela Merk)

1. Building a transmission structure: The rings of brand genesis

The brand message can only be spread if adequate structures are put in place. Trees generate rings when they grow. Year after year, new rings are added. These rings make the tree strong and solid so that it can resist the most violent storms. At the heart of the trunk is the tree's origin; the structure around it allows the tree to survive.

Every brand that wants to remain strong and grow needs to build rings around its origin so that the message can continue to grow and spread for many years (see Figure 8).

The heart: The brand creator

The brand creator is at the heart of the model. He or she created its products, built the story and filled it with his/her own spirit. In most cases, deep

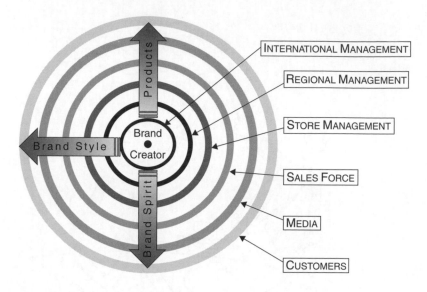

FIG 8 / **The rings of brand genesis**

passion is the biggest drive for genius creations. This passion then needs to be passed on, like the Olympic flame, from person to person, covering long distances and encountering obstacles without the flame being extinguished. During this transmission process, the flame must be protected in the most professional way and passed on throughout the various levels. Besides this, you must make sure that most people are reached within a limited period of time and on a regular basis, that they receive consistent messages and are able to provide feedback as well. Recurrent meetings on all levels are a must in order to pass on the flame to everyone. One thing is certain: a huge fire can be lit if people who are involved in the transmission process get to meet the creator him/herself: the soul of the entire idea, the origin of everyone's mission.

> *I used to work for Ralph Lauren and I can tell you one thing: if you allow salespeople from all over the world to travel to the US to meet Ralph Lauren in person, this equals 800 hours of training. To them, it is like traveling to Mecca.*
> (Arnaud Vidal, former Vice President Watches and Jewelry at Ralph Lauren and former General Manager of Audemars Piguet)

The international management ring

In order to facilitate the transmission process and make sure that the brand is developing in the right direction, carefully elaborated structures need to be put in place. The role of the international manager then becomes essential. When this function is assimilated by the brand creator him/herself, strong leadership qualities and a visionary spirit are required. The general manager's challenge is to be the brand's structuring, strategic and controlling element. He or she must work hand in hand with the creator and the board. The board includes diverse functions from marketing, human resources, training, communication to commercial functions on a strategic level. These people must fully incarnate the brand spirit and pass it on to their teams whose task is to prepare the brand message in such a way that it can be spread all across the world. The stronger their positive energy, influence and personality, the more hearts will be won during the brand transmission process.

> We all absorbed the energy we got from Alain Dominique Perrin and passed it on to our teams. This amazing energy filled the entire company and the brand Cartier as a whole.
>
> (Nathalie Banessy Monasterio,
> former Retail Development Director at Richemont)

The regional management ring

Country-specific managers, or retail directors, should be close to the brand president and the creator since they become their messengers and spokespeople in every country in which the brand is distributed. They need to embody the creator's vision, personality and style from head to toe. They should be the brand's strongest ambassadors, and must have a close relationship with the brand so that the storytelling process can be efficient and the message can be spread well. Since the creator and brand president cannot be present at all events around the globe or in all stores, since they can't interact with all of the brand's touchpoints, regional managers are crucial.

According to the brand's focus and sector, these spokespeople have different titles and their tasks vary. Depending on the brand's size, various levels of spokespeople gather around the creator: from retail or commercial brand directors to regional brand directors to country-specific managers.

The brand director's role can also be to add proximity to rather distant brand creators who are living in their world of inspiration:

> *Mrs. Prada is not very close to the field. It is therefore my role to add this human aspect, which she cannot bring along with her. Our salespeople also expect that. Mrs. Prada brings amazing collections and communication rather than proximity to the teams. It is my role to pass on her message within our organization.*
>
> (Natalie Bader, CEO of Prada France,
> former President at Fred International, former Director at Sephora)

While I was working as general manager for the makeup brand Bobbi Brown, I was impressed by the structure that was put in place in order to make sure that Bobbi's attitudes reached all stores. The brand had established the Bobbi Pro Team, a central team that worked with Bobbi Brown on product development and on the elaboration of training and sales techniques on a daily basis. All salespeople in the USA got the chance to meet with Pro Team members in order to fully absorb Bobbi Brown's spirit and charisma. As a new general manager for the German market I was also sent over to be close to the heart of the brand and absorb its essence in order to pass it on, once back dealing with my new responsibilities. You could literally feel that Bobbi's flame was being passed on during such central training sessions.

Brands need to be very careful when selecting brand representatives. Representatives should be able to embody the creator's vision quickly and naturally, and speak the creator's language without pretending to be the creator him/herself. Brand representatives should not convey arrogance when interacting with others: store managers, salespeople and customers. Unfortunately, throughout my interviews in the field, I realized that brand representatives could break the relationship between the brand and the sales force. I often heard frustrated front-line salespeople for famous luxury brands tell stories of arrogant brand representatives:

> *They totally ignore us when they enter the store since they feel superior to us. They only talk to the store manager but not to us, the simple sales force. Why should we burn for a brand that ignores us? Whenever this happens, we stop recommending the brand, we feel strongly demotivated and disappointed.*
>
> (Sales associates in a concept store)

Instead, heart-winning brand representatives are sympathetic and inspiring since they are filled with passion and are experts in the brand. They should not make any hierarchical differences when they interact with staff members in the stores. All of their contacts are important in the relationship-building process.

The store management ring

Store managers interact directly with the brand representatives; they must be able to understand the brand message and constantly transmit it to their team. They add the management component to the brand message. The more they promote this message, the stronger relationships are established with the sales force. Good store managers can greatly amplify the brand's story. However, they can also damage the process if they are not receptive to the message, if their fire does not burn.

In order to reach out to each store manager, regular meetings need to be established between the head office and the stores. A former general manager of Descamps described the multiplication process as the only way of successfully passing on the brand message to more than 300 sales-people on a regular basis:

> *I gathered all store managers every two months in order to share all brand-related issues. These meetings were a great chance to remind them of the core values, to refer to products, novelties and all activities around the brand. It was then the store managers' task to do the same with their teams.*

The sales force ring

The role of the sales force is to convey the brand message to their customers:

> *We are the priests of happiness, just like the priests who preach every Sunday about love, peace and joy. We are part of a wonderful profession where we share our convictions and feelings with others!*
> (Paul Bassène, High Jewelry Manager at Cartier)

Salespeople need to be extremely empathetic and able to identify the way they will tell the product's story. Each customer is different; they are not all receptive to the same messages. Even if there is one central story, it can be told in many ways without changing the essence. Besides the necessity of adapting the story according to the type of customer, salespeople also need to find their own way of telling it. This ensures the selling ritual stays in line with the salesperson's true character and style. Salespeople are the actors on stage that have to interpret the message so that selling remains natural. The brand message then remains credible. It is therefore crucial to find people who fit well with the brand without having to change their personality. Otherwise, it would almost be like living a double life for them and would cost managers, colleagues and salespeople a tremendous amount of energy.

The media ring

Through the media, the creator's message becomes visible to the outside world. It should reflect the brand identity in its purest state. To pass on the original vision in the most authentic way, brands need to find the right faces, words, music, atmosphere and media channels. Celebrities must be carefully chosen to be the perfect match between the creator's idea and the generated image. When done well, the media can be the biggest amplifier in the transmission process, since the brand message is made visible and creates aspirations, dreams and desires.

The customer ring

Customers are the last element in the transmission chain. Only flames that are burning strongly enough can light customers' fire. On the long path of transmission, this fire should never die out. No interruption is allowed. In the Olympic Games, that fire is lit when the flame arrives in the Olympic stadium and fills the audience – people from all over the world – with emotion. The widely visible flame is thus symbolically spread throughout the world, just like the brand's message.

2. Providing tangible tools

The first tool any brand should develop is the brand book. Even though this is the most fundamental way to capture the brand's essence and identity, the majority of brands do not invest a lot of time and effort in its development. In a structured but beautifully illustrated way, brand books need to include:

- the brand's essence
- the creator's message pointing to the origin of the brand

- the brand's history
- the brand's values, which need to be visible in all marketing tools
- the brand's expertise
- the core target group
- the graphic charter illustrating the use of the logo and the brand colors
- product and brand images
- product combinations
- merchandising guidelines indicating the way the brand should be displayed in stores.

It's an excellent exercise for brands to build their own brand books, since it forces teams to think about how they would like to see the brand as a brand builder, how salespeople should understand the brand as brand sellers and how customers should think about the brand as brand buyers. Many brands try to make savings here since they believe that salespeople don't read these books. This is a mistake, since brand books are considered among the most precious gifts a brand can give. It is almost like handing over the Bible to religious followers.

Other than brand books, there are several very efficient tools that can be used to pass on the message to salespeople, such as books in which brand creators reveal their thoughts about the brand and its visual identity, and their key messages to the world. On my first working day for Bobbi Brown I was given one of her bestsellers, the *Bobbi Brown Makeup Manual*. When I started my mission for Lacoste to build the brand's e-commerce platform, I was offered *Lacoste's Green Book*, which illustrated the brand as René Lacoste imagined it. Such books are amazing tools to offer to young salespeople once they join the company. They are one of the most useful gifts you can give in terms of igniting the salespeople's love for the brand.

Another very efficient way of passing on the flame within your organization, including within the sales force, is to internally distribute press articles that talk about your brand, products, campaigns and store openings. This important step is often forgotten, especially among salespeople, but it has maximum effect.

A few brands have started to be very creative in their way of developing tools to spread the message. One exemplary case, illustrated below, is that of Guerlain:

> *When new salespeople start working for Guerlain, we give them a starter kit or welcome-gift box on their first day of work, designed just for them. This box contains tools to guide them into the brand. Its content can change slightly according to the country or cultural differences. There is a booklet that includes anecdotes, stories surrounding the brand, actions to take and products to know. Every day the new recruit should read another page! Very important: the emotional component.*
>
> *We also developed an audio guide just like the ones you get in museums: for 45 minutes a voice speaks of Guerlain's original story, talks about its creators and describes one of our ten most emblematic products, with which everyone needs to be familiar immediately after joining the brand. Here, too, the content is slightly adapted to the country and recorded in the local language. This audio guide is very popular since it corresponds to the brand's culture: a mix of oral transmission and written facts.*
>
> *Besides, the kit contains pressed tea inscribed with our brand name. The tea is not for sale but serves to pass on emotions and the brand's history.*
>
> *The starter kit also contains little jars of honey; the honey is produced close to our production site. This item is very symbolic since it is a reminder of the origin of our brand and its logo, the imperial bee.*
>
> *Originally, we developed this kit for distributors. But due to the huge success and enthusiastic feedback we got, especially from the sales force, we decided to widen its use.*
>
> (Agnès Combes, Training Director at Chanel,
> former International Training Director at Guerlain)

3. Offering brand experience

One of the most efficient strategies to light the fire of passion for the brand in salespeople's hearts is to provide them with a full brand experience. They should get a chance to dive into the brand's universe from head to toe and get to the heart of the brand. This isn't so much brand training as it is a brand discovery or journey. Whenever salespeople tell me about their brand journeys – assuming they have had the chance to experience this – their eyes shine.

Each brand has its own universe where products are made, where research is taking place, where innovation happens. Usually, these places are the cocoon of the brand creators. So let your salespeople go and experience the belly and roots of your brand, the places where all the power comes from. Let them take in the brand's energy so that the rings of brand genesis become more and more stable and expand.

A store manager at Fendi shared her brand experience with me, which was the starting point of a strong relationship between her and the brand:

> *They allowed me to travel to Rome, the origin of Fendi. I visited the Palazzo, our flagship store, into which the head office is incorporated. There I understood why Fendi loves using yellow marble: it stands for the sunset and the amazing atmosphere when the sun is reflected on the rooftops of Rome. Then I visited the production site for fur since we are the leading brand for fur in the world. Meeting people who work closely with Silvia Fendi and Karl Lagerfeld was breathtaking. That's when I really understood the essence of the brand. It was a true discovery.*

Audemars Piguet is a great example, allowing salespeople to fully experience the brand. The country general managers select the best salespeople to visit the brand academy in Switzerland, which is located in the cradle of fine watchmaking, Le Brassus.

The selected salespeople first visit our historic museum. There, at the heart of the brand, they experience the brand's evolution since 1875 and can see masterpieces worth millions of euros.

After the visit, they meet the management team: the marketing department talks about product novelties, general management shares brand strategies, the innovation manager informs them

*about research. Through such encounters, salespeople experi-
ence the brand's international component and strength as a
whole.*

*The following day, participants visit one of the most important
production sites where over 800 watchmakers elaborate on the
most exclusive watches you can find in the marketplace today.
This is fascinating as it takes more than a year to assemble all
pieces for some watches. Salespeople meet with those who work
for more than 365 days on one watch before they can finally put
their name on a masterpiece with incredibly sophisticated watch
movements. In order to give salespeople a sense of the level of
expertise required to produce these watches, we allow them to
assemble a simple watch themselves. Salespeople who visited the
academy feel that their connection with the brand has changed.
Now they are part of the brand. They have been allowed to hear
its heartbeat before going back to their respective countries and
spreading Audemars Piguet's message.*

(Arnaud Vidal, former Vice President Watches and Jewelry at Ralph Lauren
and former General Manager of Audemars Piguet)

*In order to allow salespeople and customers to experience our
brand's rich history, we built a museum on the first floor of our
flagship store on Place Vendôme in Paris. Our brand's greatest
masterpieces are presented there as well as the entire archive,
which goes back to the brand's foundation in 1775. How many
brands still in existence can say that their customers were Louis
XVI, Napoleon, Josephine or Marie Antoinette? This museum
helps visitors to acquire better brand knowledge, gets them to
experience the brand and trace its history. Besides, it helps our
teams acquire a good general knowledge of our legacy. The
reason for building the museum here is related to the fact that the
brand's founder, Abraham-Louis Breguet, produced his watches
in the heart of Paris.*

(Emmanuel Breguet, Brand Manager of Breguet France and
in charge of the brand's heritage)

Other ideas could include organizing exhibits to reveal your brand's legacy. You can then invite your sales teams to these unique occasions where they can absorb the brand spirit:

> *When Saint Laurent organized a huge exhibit about his brand at the Grand Palais in Paris, all salespeople were invited. They felt so privileged since the exhibit opened specially for them with a guided tour during lunch hours. Each store manager could invite his team. Absorbing the essence of the brand in such amazing surroundings was a fantastic experience.*
>
> (Jean-Charles Champey, former Store Manager at Yves Saint Laurent)

Visiting a showroom when new collections come out is another effective way of transmitting brand experience. This allows the sales teams to view the new creations before they are shown to the public, and gives salespeople the message that "you are VIP to us."

Instead of inviting salespeople to visit the cradle and heart of the brand, why not have it come to their stores? Some watchmakers have already started recognizing the importance of bringing the worlds of production and sales closer together. In order to strengthen brand relationships both for salespeople and for their customers, taking the brand's essence and expertise directly to the stores makes perfect sense. This is especially true in industries where after-sales services are part of the business, such as in the watch or car industries. Both cars and watches need to be revised, changed, repaired and checked regularly. You don't buy a car or a watch for a lifetime without having to repair it. When the product is sold, the salespeople know that they will see their client again. So why not include watchmakers, bag producers, fragrance designers and jewelry artists in the stores? This would allow salespeople to feel the brand's heartbeat every day and to expand their expertise: they would evolve from being a salesperson to becoming a sales doctor, diagnosing damaged products before handing them over to the experts.

Allowing salespeople to enter into your brand universe by having them meet with personalities who are passionate about their activity is another possibility. If you are in the wine business, you can organize meetings with people who manage their own vineyards, if you are selling perfumes, your sales force can meet with "noses," and if you are selling watches related to aviation, introduce them to pilots:

> *It's very interesting to meet exceptional pilots, experts in aviation and commanding officers! It is a question of passion. When we feel their deep passion, we quickly get infected too and the feeling stays for a long time deep inside our hearts.*
>
> (Store manager at a high-end watchmaking brand)

4. Brand revival: Celebrating a legacy

Brand anniversaries are great moments at which brand managers can remind their sales force and customers of the brand's legacy and its creators. They are unique opportunities to look back on the brand's origin and evolution. Reconnecting with the past is essential in a brand's life cycle because it allows you to step back and reflect before looking ahead. It is also the perfect time to communicate your brand to a new generation of salespeople who may have lost that direct emotional link. Customers will rediscover their brand with nostalgia and salespeople will definitely be affected too.

There are multiple ways of celebrating such historical moments in a brand's life. One efficient strategy is to revive past creations. Redesigning them lights the brand's fire again, animating the brand's soul and giving salespeople a good reason to talk about its rich past.

> *For the 75-year anniversary of Fred, they re-created a former collection called 'Pain de Sucre.' This collection was made out of the most beautiful precious stones, in all colors, from South America. This is where Fred Samuel used to live. The masterpieces included jewelry that went from accessible to high-end prices.*
>
> (Fred sales associate)

Heart-winner 3: Let the fire burn!

Once the flame has been kindled, once it is beautifully burning and gradually transforms into a huge fire, it is important to preserve it. If we don't take care of the flame, it won't burn for long. Then, all the effort to light it will have been wasted.

Most salespeople who have developed strong relationships with their brands truly believe that they are superior to other brands. Their daily work gives them pleasure and they are enthusiastic when interacting with the brand and the customer. In science, this kind of motivation is called "intrinsic motivation."[1] It is stimulated from within and is deeply related to salespeople's emotions. Intrinsic motivation keeps salespeople attached to their brand for a long time even when competitors offer them more money. It is the kind of motivation you want to generate in a salesperson's heart.

Since the brand creator plays such an important role in the process of lighting the fire, transition periods are real tests of lasting brand love. When creators disappear, there is a real danger that the fire that is burning within the brand's sales force will be extinguished. For that reason, the original brand creator's succession must be carefully managed in order to guarantee continuity. Otherwise, the flame will diminish and die. When Karl Lagerfeld succeeded Coco Chanel he managed to maintain her legacy: a genius succeeded to a genius. There are also examples where fires that were almost out were able to burn again thanks to new charismatic creators taking over, as we saw in the case of John Galliano for Dior or Phoebe Philo for Céline.

> *I experienced the arrival of Phoebe Philo when she took over the creative direction of Céline. There was this mind-blowing 'wow effect' among employees, salespeople and customers. This alone motivated everyone to remain within the brand.*
>
> (Jean-Charles Champey, former Retail Excellence Program Manager at Céline)

Yet the existence of charismatic creators is not the only method by which to keep fires burning. One of the most efficient tools is training staff, including store managers, on a regular basis and constantly reminding them of the brand's history, its products and its philosophy. This allows them to experience the brand not only once in their career but as often as possible, giving them the feeling of actively living with it.

---

[1] L. W. Porter and E. E. Lawler (1968) *Managerial Attitudes and Performance.* Homewood, IL: Richard D. Irwin, Inc.

As opposed to intrinsic motivation, extrinsic motivation emerges through external means such as rewards and remuneration. Interestingly, the motivation researcher E. L. Deci found that external factors such as rewards and evaluations reduced feelings of autonomy and undermined intrinsic motivation.[2]

Over the course of my interviews among salespeople, I also found that money killed emotions. When the emphasis is put on sales objectives and compensation systems the emotional component linking salespeople to their brands decreases (Figure 9). Even worse, badly managed remuneration systems extinguish burning hearts. The sales process shifts from an emotional process to a purely cognitive one and relationships become extremely fragile.

However, this does not mean that sales control systems are not important. On the contrary, they are essential in order to stimulate the entire team

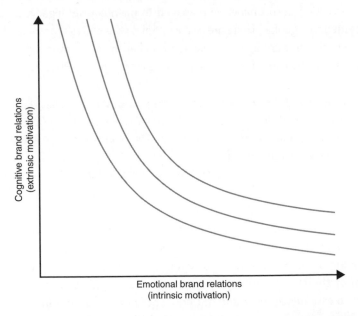

FIG 9 / **Emotional versus cognitive relationships between the sales force and the brand**

[2] E. L. Deci (1971) "Effects of externally mediated rewards on intrinsic motivation." *Journal of Personal and Social Psychology*, 18, 105–15.

and to keep the sales ritual dynamic. Sales control systems are seen as fundamental to the sales profession rather than being a factor meant to strengthen emotional bonds between salespeople and the brand. This is congruent with another phenomenon we know from motivational research. Herzberg's "Two Factor Theory" distinguishes between two types of factors:[3] motivational factors that reinforce motivation, and hygiene factors that don't contribute to motivation but, if absent, can generate huge dissatisfaction. The results of my interviews clearly showed that sales control and compensation systems were taken for granted but didn't light the fire of salespeople. However, if they were badly managed, burning fires could be extinguished.

It is therefore important to implement effective sales control and compensation systems. The hundreds of interviews I conducted with salespeople and their managers allowed me to identify strengths and weaknesses in existing compensation systems. Even though these systems are very

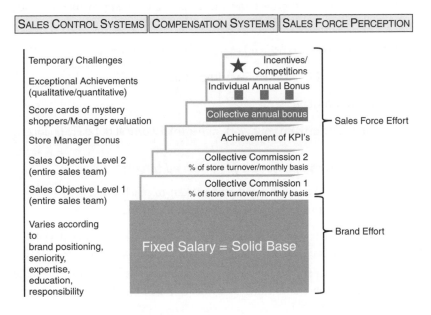

FIG 10 The control–compensation podium

---

[3] F. Herzberg, B. Mausner and B. Snyderman (1959) *The Motivation to Work.* New York: Wiley.

difficult to standardize due to different external factors such as the sales environment, the sector, the life cycle of the brand, the budget or the competition, I want to offer a model that seems best suited to maintaining a good relationship between salespeople and their brands (Figure 10).

Fixed salary: The solid base

The base of the control–compensation podium is the fixed salary that is paid to each salesperson once a month. This indicates that the brand expects all its salespeople to offer an excellent quality of service. In service-intense industries such as luxury, I particularly recommend setting fixed-base pay as high as possible, and reducing commission-based pay to a minimum. The fixed rate should vary by industry sector, seniority, expertise, education level and the management responsibility a salesperson holds.

Interviews with the sales force allowed me to identify what kind of messages brands indirectly evoke when paying high fixed salaries:

"We are looking for the best sales force and are willing to pay for your services!"

"We trust in your expertise and expect excellence in return."

"Not only sellout but also service is important."

"We want you to stay!"

"We want you to focus on your work rather than worry about daily finances!"

Commissions: A compensation for achieved targets

The following steps, which need to be taken to reach the higher revenue levels, are meant to compensate a salesperson's effort.

The first two steps can be reached by achieving sales targets that have been fixed by management, ideally for the entire sales team. The advantage of the two-level system is that you can announce both one achievable objective and a more ambitious one. This is more stimulating than setting only one target.

First of all, it is important to determine realistic and achievable goals in order to kindle an emotional flame with regard to commission. In the particular case they related, the sales objectives were sometimes so high that they seemed impossible to reach. In the middle of each month the teams calculated whether they could still achieve the goal. If it seemed unattainable, they dropped everything out of sheer frustration. It is, therefore, very important to fix realistic and motivating goals. Of course, sales managers want to boost sales and are always concerned about reaching the end-of-the-month target. Yet sales objectives that are too high generate stress and put pressure on the relationship between the brand and its sales force.

In boutique or department store environments, paying commissions for the entire team rather than for the individual person is recommended. Collective commissions foster team spirit; individual commissions generate war on the floor. Most of the interviewed salespeople agreed with this. They hate individual commissions and clearly favor the collective approach since it stimulates teamwork, service quality, overall efficiency and justice.

> *When I worked for Dior, our commission was team-based. We all wanted to help each other to achieve high sales. When you work in a department store, the stock is not always available at the counter. While one salesperson explains the products to the customer, another colleague can back them up by using sales arguments, while a third one gets the products from the stock room. Someone else will take care of payment and another person will wrap up the product to make a nice gift. If commissions were paid for each individual person we would not want to collaborate and succeed together.*
>
> (Dior sales associate)

In addition, collective commission systems are more adapted to the sales reality than individual systems, since selling not only requires skill but also luck.

> *You can be the best salesperson on earth, spend time and energy explaining the brand but the potential customer may be unable to pay for any product on offer in the boutique. Another salesperson, however, might find herself in front of a rich Chinese customer willing to purchase five bags in a row without even needing any help. Who invested more effort? Would it be right to pay higher commissions to the person who simply sold more? Under such conditions we would only be interested in identifying customers with purchasing potential, would behave like*

sharks attacking wealthy-looking clients and would forget about team spirit and our love for the brand.

(Sales associate at a luxury accessory brand)

Individual-based commission systems create internal competition and generate the feeling among salespeople that service before selling is not necessary and that only figures count. In the luxury industry especially, highly professional service is the most important part of the sales ritual. Given this reality, the commission proportion should be kept as small as possible in order to reinforce the importance of service.

Paying high commissions is counterproductive in the luxury industry. All customers must be served with equal excellence no matter the amount they purchase. If you start reinforcing commissions, salespeople will only focus on rich customers willing to spend €10,000 instead of €100. In our department store I notice that brands paying individual commission rates provoke incredible tensions within their teams. Not only do customers feel these tensions, but they also get the impression that the service level is low if they do not appear wealthy enough. The consequence: they come to the conclusion that they are considered not good enough for the brand and leave. Clearly, salespeople who are attracted by commission rates cannot love the brand they sell. And if they don't love their brand they won't stay. Any competitor offering higher compensation systems will make them jump ship.

(Alexandre Ferragu, former Retail Sales Manager Luxury and Accessories at Printemps)

The bonus: A compensation for excellence

The first type of bonus should be put in place for store managers and based on great achievements, especially relating to their management skills and key performance indicators (KPIs). These bonuses could be paid on a monthly basis. Store managers would then be stimulated to constantly motivate their teams, foster team spirit and drive their store to sales excellence.

The second bonus system, the collective bonus, could be addressed to salespeople and paid at the end of the year for outstanding achievements.

A mystery shopper's evaluation could be the control system for collective bonuses. Qualitative elements could therefore enter into the evaluation system such as:

- service level
- customer loyalty
- sense of welcome
- clothes/uniform
- physical appearance
- merchandising
- shop cleanliness
- product knowledge
- brand knowledge
- team spirit
- training and knowledge transfer.

The control system for individual bonuses must be reserved for outstanding individual achievements, such as very important sales levels. Although this is hard to practice, the most effective way would be to link the salesperson's pay as closely as possible to the amazing performance that triggered the bonus.

> *When I was managing Cartier, I made sure that the bonuses for exceptional performance were paid as soon as the results were out. Sometimes we managed to pay them on the same evening as the person's achievement. Unfortunately, this is not possible any more, since organizations are too large. This compensation system, however, was highly efficient. Today, I still practice this method within the small and mid-sized companies I own.*
>
> *The compensation system is different for sales representatives. In this case, it is important to have individual commissions and apply the same commission rate.*
>
> (Alain Dominique Perrin, Non-Executive Director at Richemont Group, former President of Cartier International, President of EFMD (European Foundation for Management Development) and President of EDC (École des Dirigeants et Créateurs d'Entreprises))

Individual bonuses were paid to salespeople who had successfully undertaken very long sales processes and achieved high turnover, selling jewelry for over €60,000 to one customer, for instance. In these cases, the sales process had to be carefully planned over the course of several months. This occurs, for example, when rich families from the Middle East want to purchase tailor-made jewelry. They don't come to your stores. You have to go and see them in their hotel room at night. After having presented your work, you get their feedback and have to work on the masterpiece again, make new designs and get the rarest precious stones. One of the best Cartier salespeople during my time took over two and a half years to conclude the sales process and managed to sell several millions of euros of products in the end.

(Nathalie Banessy Monasterio,
former Retail Development Director at Richemont)

Incentives: Punctual compensation systems

In order to stimulate salespeople temporarily, incentives can be put in place. However, these can be destructive if they are not designed in the right way. So how can we identify incentives that stoke the fire?

The best tools are mechanisms that foster team spirit or that promote a general understanding of the brand. They should be fun to experience. For that reason, there are no limits to creativity when designing an original promotion campaign to tighten the relationship between salespeople and their brand.

I was among the finalists of a competition that was organized in four steps: we first had to send a motivation letter to top management. We then made a video about Fendi's brand values, which are creativity, modernity, baroque and dualism, and we had to find these values in our own town. The third step was to send in three recommendation letters written by our best clients. The last step was an interview at a worldwide level. The best 40 finalists out of 2000 were invited, which allowed us to meet our counterparts from Japan, China, the USA and other countries. The exchange of best practices was simply amazing. These kinds of competitions are so stimulating that those who were not selected try their luck again the following year.

(Fendi store manager)

It is not easy for salespeople who work for luxury brands to sell products that exceed their own purchasing capacities by far. In order to avoid a certain frustration factor, winning luxury items from the brand as a team is an excellent stimulator and helps to strengthen the relationship between the salesperson and the brand.

Below you see the main compensation systems that might lead to a rupture of the sales force–brand relationship:

Table 1   Compensation systems that break sales force–brand relationships

Compensation Strategy	Consequence/Sales force perception
Low fixed salary, high commission	Impression of exploitation Short-term vision Low brand contribution Sales are more important than service
Objectives that are too ambitious	Pressure Demotivation Abandonment of objectives
Individual commission	Strife Internal competition No team spirit Impression of unfairness
Compensations that are too complicated	Confusion Lack of understanding for the field

2.2   How to help salespeople identify with your brand

Heart-winner 4: Develop human values!

Brands that spread a positive spirit can win salespeople's hearts and thus foster brand relationships. This positive spirit has to incorporate the brand's core values. These values reflect the personality, charisma, attitude and character of the brand creator or the person who made the main contribution to what the brand is today.

Nathalie Banessy Monasterio, former Retail Development Director at Richemont Group, underlines the importance of strong brand values by using the example of Cartier:

> *Perfection, the desire for excellence, detail and honesty are the inner values of the brand, which are visible in every step it takes.*

> *Cartier transmits these values to its salespeople. Even the company restaurant called 'le Petit Café' is magnificent, with beautifully folded napkins decorating the tables and delicious food. Every detail is important. Even the toilets are pretty. Salespeople are respected in all they do: changing rooms look luxurious, the uniforms they wear are of the highest quality and they are refunded for expenses at the hairdressers or at nail studios.*

A luxury brand with strong relationship potential must be generous. Show your brand's gratitude, encourage your salespeople to be helpful and give them little gifts to demonstrate these values.

> *I strongly believe in luxury being directly related to generosity. A luxury brand becomes desirable when it is generous. I will never forget the time when our team from the boutique in Faubourg Saint-Honoré helped a man in a wheelchair, right across from the Hermès store. His wheel was broken. So they decided to repair the wheel for free without asking his name, destination, customer profile or offering him any products. A month later, the man wrote to the team to say how thankful he was for the generous help they offered him that day. Reading the letter they learned that this man had been a loyal customer to the brand for years. Luxury should not be selfish but generous. It is in the gestures.*
> **(Christian Blanckaert, Professor in Luxury Management at ESCP Europe and former CEO of Hermès Sellier and Hermès International)**

Shaping human brand values is not enough. Values need to be embodied by those who are managing the brands and their salespeople. These people are the role models who represent the values in person. Only then can the identification process be accomplished. It's similar to being in marriage: a couple can last if each person's values are clearly expressed and aligned. A mismatch in value perceptions and expectations is likely to lead to divorce.

In order to strengthen the bond between salespeople and their brand, the values of salespeople, brands and managers need to be in harmony with one another (Figure 11).

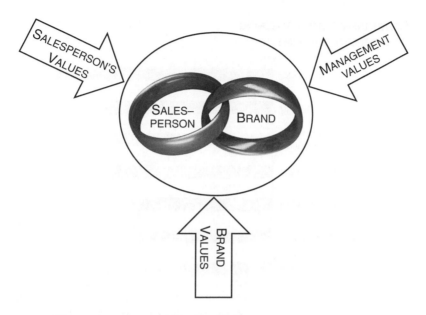

FIG 11 / The value system in sales force–brand relationships

What kind of management behavior and values lead to the most positive impact on sales force–brand identification?

From my sales force interviews, I was able to establish the following ranking of management characteristics. In this study, salespeople were asked to mention the most important characteristics managers should possess in order to create strong relationships with their employees (Figure 12).

Seventy percent of the respondents identify with the brand if their manager acts like a role model. This means managers should embody the brand's values and respect the guidelines that they impose on their teams, among others: reliability, honesty and punctuality.

> *A good manager is honest with his team and would not do whatever he strictly forbids his team from doing. Our current manager constantly arrives after the store's opening hour, goes on Skype during business hours, takes many days off and does not treat us with respect. Consequently, our motivation for the brand is down, sales have dropped, we are not in line with the brand anymore.*
>
> (Sales associate at a luxury fashion brand)

RELATIONSHIP STRENGTHENING MANAGEMENT QUALITIES

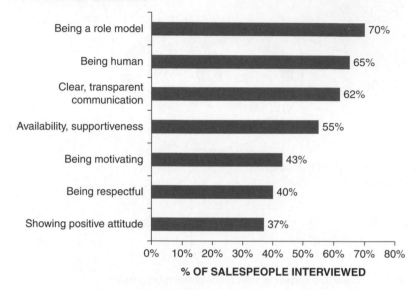

FIG 12 / **A manager's qualities to foster sales force–brand relationships**

(Results from PhD research Michaela Merk based upon 400 sales force interviews)

Although managers should be seen as role models who can be respected, they also need to display human traits. Sixty-five percent of the interviewed salespeople expect their managers to be human, just and empathetic. To them, "being human" does not exclude sticking to strict management guidelines. Shouting at team members, for instance, is perceived as a sign of weakness and incompetence. What they appreciate is when their managers show concern for their team's well-being instead of merely asking about target fulfillment or product knowledge.

> *I felt estranged from the brand as a result of my management's lack of human values. I got the impression that no one cared about me as a person. They only asked me to master all products perfectly, to control stock levels, to achieve sales targets. But where was I in this system?*
>
> (Sales associate for a premium fashion brand)

The first encounter between salespeople and their managers is a crucial moment in the relationship-building process. Salespeople will feel at home within their brand if their manager gives them the feeling of being welcome as a person and not just as a number-crunching robot:

> *I loved the first encounter with the president of our brand. She was accessible, human, always in a good mood and smiling. It is very motivating to be recruited by a manager of this kind. However, every change in management endangers these values. If my personal values are not in line with management's values, I look for new opportunities.*
>
> (Fred sales associate)

This feeling of being welcome is related to sales management communication, which must be clear and transparent (according to 62 percent of those interviewed). Salespeople want to know the direction in which they need to go without having to deviate too many times. Modern technology like e-mails and the telephone are useful in this process but do not replace personal exchanges with managers.

> *We must not dehumanize our relationship with management. Drinking coffee with my manager and getting one-to-one feedback from her is essential. Nothing is worse than silence or dehumanized communication. The risk is particularly high in countries, like the USA, with large geographic distances. Lack of communication damages our relationships with the brand.*
>
> (Cartier store manager)

A brand that stands for strong human values facilitates the identification process. It is, however, not only the managers and sales representatives who are able to transmit these values. Such values can also be passed on, on an even wider scale, by carefully selected famous spokespeople who embody these values and represent a certain lifestyle and attitude.

> *My identification with Lancôme became even stronger when Isabella Rossellini, who is such a magnificent celebrity, was chosen to embody the French fundamentals of esthetics and refinement. She released incredible authenticity and sympathy, which is fully in line with the brand creator's intention. She made the brand accessible.*
>
> (Sandrine Sabathé, Sales Representative at Lancôme)

Human brand values can also be lived and shared by implementing common activities related to these values. These activities promote team-building but also have the effect of transmission, of consciously living your brand's values. Too many brands "demonstrate" what they stand for by simply writing their values on a piece of paper. But there is no sense in writing these down if you do not act on them!

Lawrence Grodzicki, Demandware Project Management Director, former E-commerce Project Manager and Retail Systems Expert at Timberland, says:

Timberland is more than a company that just sells footwear and apparel. It has a broader corporate and social agenda, rooted in the heritage of the once family-owned business. Former CEO Jeff Swartz believes that doing well and doing good are inextricably linked; the belief that companies who do well by being profitable have a social obligation to do good by giving back to the community. Under Jeff's tenure, Timberland employees were given 40 paid hours a year to perform community service, and the company organizes many of these events.

Let me give you an example: when Hurricane Katrina hit New Orleans and destroyed countless homes, Timberland employees built replacement homes for the victims. Building materials were delivered to our corporate headquarters in New Hampshire, and, on a regular workday, hundreds of employees gathered together and constructed walls for new homes. The walls were shipped to New Orleans where they were assembled on site, shortening the time to needed to create a finished home.

Besides doing good for others, this project had many benefits for employees. Non-managers had opportunities to demonstrate leadership by acting as event organizers. Employees who usually never got to work together were able to collaborate and build new relationships. And we felt the joy that comes from helping others, which is itself a wonderful reward.

However, there is one other benefit that cannot be discounted. When a company regularly demonstrates its commitment to its values, the employee feels part of something larger. The

> *employee's job is not just a job, but a job that has a real impact and makes a difference in someone's life. A Timberland company motto is, 'Pull on your boots and make a difference.' We did. That's just how the company encouraged us to act.*

Heart-winner 5: Let them feel at home!

The store, especially a brand's own boutique, is the place that most represents the brand's values. This is where the brand can show all its facets, where it demonstrates to the world what it stands for, which materials it loves, which colors and shapes it prefers, and which kind of atmosphere it wants to create: cosy, charming, stylish, modern, trashy, luxurious, vintage, crazy, girly, pure and so on.

The better a brand succeeds in transposing its values into its sale venues, the more it helps salespeople identify with their store and the brand. Symbols that represent the brand's identity should, therefore, be at the heart of all merchandising tools. They allow a boutique to be unique. Louis Vuitton reminds people of its origins – producing trunks at the beginning of the 19th century – by displaying models of the first masterpieces in its Champs-Élysées flagship store. Meanwhile, Lacoste keeps a visual memory of René in most of its boutiques:

> *Our salespeople love telling the story of the brand creation since it is true and authentic. As a permanent reminder we wanted to integrate this authenticity into our stores by putting up posters of René Lacoste in various spots. This helps our sales force constantly connect with the brand's origin, its founder.*
>
> (Alexandre Fauvet, former Executive Vice President at Lacoste)

Yet making use of iconic brand symbols is not enough to help salespeople identify with the brand for which they work. Companies also need to demonstrate that they understand a salesperson's profession by designing boutiques in a way that is perfectly adapted to their daily tasks and that allows them to feel at home. Many salespeople shared with me past negative experiences of having to work in stores that were totally inappropriate for their needs. Few of them stayed since they simply could not connect with their brand. Salespeople spend more time in their boutique than at their own home. The sales environment therefore needs to be designed to facilitate the relationship between the salesperson and the brand, and to allow salespeople to fulfill their sales task without encountering too many obstacles along the way. This is important both from an aesthetic and from a practical perspective. Whenever brands or retailers design a new store, it is as important to think about the salesperson's environment, as it is to carefully reflect on the customer "surface." Since salespeople have to work closely together in often small spaces, it is recommended that areas be allocated exclusively to one salesperson. Salespeople will identify more easily with the brand and the sales environment if they are given personal space in their stores. It is only human to identify and define one's personal territory. In the watch and jewelry business, sales areas such as little tables can be reserved for a specific salesperson.

> *Every salesperson had his personal table. Whenever they were present in the store, this is where they sat to communicate with the customer. When I was working on the new concept for the Cartier boutiques, I spent hours*

ILL 5 / Feeling at home!

(Source: Albert Dessinateur for Michaela Merk)

watching and imitating salespeople just to understand their gestures: How often is he sitting, standing, turning? Which tools are required?

(Nathalie Banessy Monasterio,
former Retail Development Director at Richemont)

Unfortunately, many places only focus on the areas visible to the outside world and do not put as much effort on the areas "behind-the-scenes." For example, a luxury department store invested millions of euros to renovate the sales area and the building's exterior, creating a stunningly beautiful store. However, all spaces dedicated to salespeople were totally neglected, such as areas where they could change, relax and eat. Even in such places, they should get the feeling of being as precious as customers, they should be reminded whom they work for, they should be proud of their working environment and simply feel at home. An actor can give a better performance if he can prepare himself in a cozy room backstage, a sportsman is more likely to beat the record if he has the proper facilities to warm up in before the competition. In sales, there is no difference.

The first impression counts. For a salesperson, the moment of truth is often during the interview in the recruitment process. This is when a small inner flame for the brand can blossom forth into a large one.

I will never forget the magic moment when I entered into the Cartier boutique for my interview to become a salesperson. I had never stepped into such a luxurious store in all my life. Not only was the place incredibly beautiful, but the welcome was also very warmhearted. When I went through the door, I was immediately reassured by the smile of the security guard inviting me to sit down while he called the store manager. I felt as if I had entered into a very pleasant, respectful, warm atmosphere, which corresponded to my character. I felt at home. Today, eight years later, I still remember all the little details from my first encounter with Cartier, the drink I was offered, the magazine I got. It felt like an extraordinary moment.

(Cartier store manager)

The boutiques of Frédéric Malle and Dries Van Noten have a lot in common. They want to present the products in a very personal and cozy environment, reflecting the taste of their creators. This can even go as far as finding personal objects of Frédéric and Dries in their boutiques. No doubt, the sofa is the most efficient object at giving comfort, and it appears in several stores for both brands. This helps to establish a private relationship between the salespeople and their brand. Many of our salespeople get so strongly attached to their point of sale that they keep talking about 'my boutique.' At the beginning, we had many salespeople who rotated from store to store. But in the end most of them preferred dedicating themselves to one specific place. They don't want to be in 'the other's store.' This feeling is certainly fostered by the fact that all of our boutiques have a different merchandising design. Besides, being attached to one store enables them to be so familiar with their sales environment that they can fully concentrate on the brand without losing time elsewhere.

(Sylvie Coumau, General Manager of Editions de Parfums Frédéric Malle, former Development Director of Dries Van Noten)

The atmosphere of "being at home" can also be created by the use of a specific style in decoration. Flowers, pieces of art or furniture, for instance, play a very important role in this respect. The role of these artifacts is to allow the salesperson to feel home and to make the customer feel at ease. The main goal of this merchandising strategy is to give the customer the impression of being at a good friend's place where he or she is always welcome, rather than in a commercial environment.

Flowers are important for women. They contribute to creating a cozy atmosphere and give you the impression of being in a beautiful apartment. Antique furniture and paintings, which have nothing to do with fashion, make you feel home and don't give you the impression of being in a commercial space. Dries Van Noten chose this decoration because it corresponded to his style and in order to avoid customers feeling like they entered into a fashion space. In his boutiques, you'll always find a sofa. As a hostess, this is where I received my customers. I spent a lot of time sitting on this sofa. When customers entered the boutique, I first asked them to take a seat and offered them a drink. Once they were sitting, we showed them the collection instead of asking the customer to follow the salesperson throughout the store. All of a sudden, the customer almost became like a friend, which can be both positive and negative. On one hand, an incredible proximity can be established between the customer and the sales associate, on the other hand some salespeople cross the line and go one step too far. If this happens, it is very bad and can be damaging for the brand since it gives rise to gossip.

(Shayda de Bary, former Store Manager at Dries Van Noten)

Merchandising can be of great help to salespeople in order to identify with their brand: it provides reference marks. Nevertheless, if nothing changes over time, salespeople become bored and blasé from stagnation, and no longer notice their surroundings or products. Who wants to work for a brand that never changes its face? It is therefore important to bring movement to your points of sale, without modifying the selling ritual or core elements: change shop window decorations, find creative product exposures and integrate new products. Sometimes, salespeople only begin to see products again when you change their placement. Merchandising dynamics maintain the excitement level for the brand and allow emotional ties to be strengthened.

Another way of making salespeople feel at home is to compose unique music for their stores to which they can relate. Music, if well composed and well explained, can have a very strong unifying character.

After having developed the Sephora store music, I wanted the salespeople to understand how we composed it and why. I very much believe in the pedagogical approach. I explained how the music was built by dissociating every single layer: I first let them hear the heartbeat. Then, when emotions are added, you can hear the breath that sounds like wind blowing through trees. Once you combine all the layers, you get the end result. An amazing emotional moment takes place when you explain things like that in front of 700 people. The audience had fully understood the music and therefore identified with it. It is theirs, and it is still played in the stores.

(Natalie Bader, CEO of Prada France,
former President at Fred International, former Director at Sephora)

Organization, as well as decoration and equipment, are important in order for salespeople and customers to feel at home in a boutique. If, for budget reasons, stores use fewer staff than are required to serve the customer properly, salespeople will find themselves executing tasks that do not directly add value to their core competence: such as cleaning or security. If this happens, they can feel exploited by their brand or frustrated because they aren't using their skills properly and have less time for their customers. In the high-end luxury business particularly, the customer should never be left alone during the sales process. For that reason, some brands in the watches and jewelry segment have introduced positions such as the stock manager; they bring the merchandise to the salesperson. Salespeople then do not need to leave their customer in order to get the desired product from storage. Another crucial moment in the sales process is payment. Paying hurts. While it is a salesperson's task in the luxury business to make the customer dream, it is better to have a different staff member who is specifically dedicated to the vulnerable moment of paying. Consequently, the salesperson can still preserve the dreamworld by, for instance, preparing the gift bag as the purchase is rung up. These kinds of organizational structures help salespeople identify with their specific role and the brand they represent.

If your salespeople feel comfortable in their boutique, there is a strong likelihood they will be able to make your customers feel at home too.

I always tell my customers that our boutique is their home. And I also keep saying that they shaped this home. That's why we respect our customers so much. They step into our store and share their sorrows. Recently, a lady told me how sad she felt after the death of her husband. This is a place where she feels comfortable and where people listen to her. The work we are doing in sales is a very human task.

(Paul Bassène, High Jewelry Manager at Cartier)

Heart-winner 6: Foster team spirit!

The more you succeed in building real team spirit among your salespeople, the better they will relate to your brand. The stronger the ties of your salespeople with the brand, the nicer the overall atmosphere generated in your store. Customers are extremely sensitive to such atmosphere. They can detect if a team plays together or against each other. A positive store atmosphere will immediately translate into customer satisfaction and higher turnover (Figure 13).

Good salespeople are relationship people. They love to exchange, to communicate, to share and to live key social moments. Salespeople get discouraged when they go to work in the morning knowing that they don't get along with their colleagues.

ILL 6 / **Yes we can!**

(Source: Albert Dessinateur for Michaela Merk)

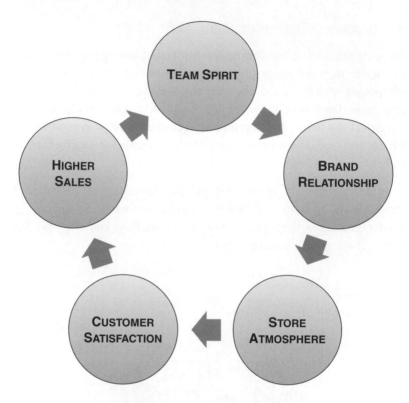

FIG 13   The impact of team spirit on brand relationships

A uniform is a visible element that unites the team. It's similar to being in a sports competition where a team wears a specific uniform that stands for the club or the country. When members of a sales team wear a uniform, it is a visible statement of the brand they represent.

> *Loving the team uniform is equal to loving your brand, which is equal to loving your team.*
> Alain Dominique Perrin, Non-Executive Director at Richemont Group,
> former President of Cartier International,
> President of EFMD (European Foundation for Management Development)
> and President of EDC (École des Dirigeants et Créateurs d'Entreprises)

> *Once you are dressed from head to toe in clothes from your brand, it is much easier to champion this brand. This is particularly true if the*

brand has a very specific style, such as Sonia Rykiel. The style is clearly defined, like a science, fully in line with what the customers want. There are women among the customers who are like mini Rykiels. They enter the boutique and always request the same type of clothes, chosen for their comfort and style. Our best customer exclusively wears Rykiel and spends a fortune. At Miu Miu, all members of the sales force wore a uniform in line with the current look. We could choose among two to three combinations of shoes, trousers, dresses and tops. Wearing the same outfit fosters a sense of identification with the brand. When we gathered in team or management meetings, we were all dressed the same. This helped us to feel part of one family. The relationship between store manager and salespeople thus becomes more obvious: the latter will focus even more on the manager's messages if he or she is giving an example.

(Shayda de Bary, Store Manager at Sonia Rykiel,
former Store Manager at Dries Van Noten and Miu Miu)

All the salespeople I interviewed agreed: the most efficient tool to unite the teams and tighten their ties with the brand and the company is to meet together on a regular basis. This is a unique opportunity to exchange notes on best practices, pass on strategic messages, and inform about product launches or other company-related issues. In these team meetings, the flame can be passed on, not only from top management to the salespeople but also among members of the sales teams.

Whenever I get the chance to meet the salespeople who made their career in the prestigious area around Place Vendôme, I try to learn from them. They are so passionate about the brand and all the other brands they have worked for. It is amazing to see how professional they are. You can learn so much from them.

(Fred sales associate)

However, when you organize events, meetings or seminars, don't forget to include all relevant staff. Failure to do this is usually perceived as an extremely negative act and is taken very personally by those overlooked, creating negative feelings of favoritism and destroying any sense of belonging with your brand. Before you invite, ask closely related people at the lower level to check your list of attendees. Never compose such a list on your own without having it checked.

Organizing dinners, weekends or any kind of activity that unites teams is crucial to creating lasting positive team spirit and a strong relationship with our brands. I often invited my sales teams to my castle. They loved it because they received a great welcome and because they got to know me even better as a person. I believe it is very important for my teams to discover me to be a simple and accessible person and not an untouchable phantom. I am actually a pretty straightforward man.

Since I used to play a lot of rugby, I also organized rugby matches among our teams. This fosters sportsmanship and fair play. I also like using rugby as an example to my team, since this is the sport that taught me about team spirit, which is necessary to win. In rugby you cannot win alone. Just as in military, in an army, you never win a war on your own. You always need a team and a captain.

What else did I do to foster team spirit? Well, during the international trade show for high-end watchmaking (SIHH = Salon International de la Haute Horlogerie), which I created 22 years ago, I had them, together with their best customers, flown there in my private plane. The show lasted one week so many salespeople could attend. It was just a question of organization. So, the plane was going back and forth between Le Bourget in France and Geneva several times a day.

What is important to take into consideration: carefully deliberate whom you are going to invite. If you forget to invite someone who should have been invited, this creates frustration and demotivation. And demotivated people are useless; you end up needing to lay them off, which is costly to the corporation in every aspect. You should therefore always have your guest list validated by someone who knows the structures of your business perfectly.

(Alain Dominique Perrin, Non-Executive Director at Richemont Group,
former President of Cartier International,
President of EFMD (European Foundation for Management Development)
and President of EDC (École des Dirigeants et Créateurs d'Entreprises))

Attending trade shows as a team is a great opportunity for staff to learn together about future trends. In all industry sectors and most geographic regions there are trade shows, thus making the organization of such trips possible wherever a particular store is situated. Furthermore, if your brand has a presence at an international trade show – even if this is merely in the form of a small booth – it allows your sales teams to view the brand in a more global context. They realize that the brand they are working for has an international reputation.

Whatever form of get-together you choose, it will help generate among staff a feeling of belonging to a huge happy family, who share one common goal: the success of the brand.

> *Salespeople are usually joyful people. It is important for them to be happy in order to make their customers happy. One year, Hermès decided to encourage our sales teams to sing together. Music unites! Every store had collective singing lessons and could choose their preferred genre: rock, classic or any other style. During this year, which we called the year of music, you could hear sales teams sing together in stores all across the world. The idea was to sing together and have fun. At the end of the year there was a big finale in each country, at which the sales teams performed their songs on stage. I assisted at the singing contest in France, which took place in the Buddha Bar in Paris. To everyone's surprise, I dressed up as a rock star and performed a song by Laurent Voulzy. I did this to show them that those in top management are also committed, can have fun and identify with their staff.*
> (Christian Blanckaert, Professor in Luxury Management at ESCP Europe and former CEO of Hermès Sellier and Hermès International)

Heart-winner 7: Show them where to go!

How can salespeople identify with their brand if they do not even know the brand's destination? Salespeople need to know what their goal is. These targets can be, among others:

- monetary, expressing a sales target
- ethic, reinforcing specific brand values
- structural, concerning the product portfolio

ILL 7 / **Following the leader into the battlefield!**

(Source: Albert Dessinateur for Michaela Merk)

- geographic, heading toward a geographic expansion
- customer focused, aiming at attracting new customers or maintaining existing ones
- competition oriented, identifying the brand's biggest enemies.

These "enemies" can be brands to which your brand stands in direct or indirect competition.

> *You need to look for your enemies, eliminate them, outdo them, be better than they are. It is important to constantly make your salespeople hungry for competition. Without competition and competitors, a salesperson is lost. These elements tie them to your brand since your brand is in danger. I told them to defend Cartier when competitors got too close. I wanted them to fight like in a rugby match, like in a war. This stirs them up, this creates the most incredible motivation. My biggest competitors are counterfeits. I was fighting against them in numerous legal processes; I put many people in prison as a result of illegal brand copying.*
>
> Alain Dominique Perrin, Non-Executive Director at Richemont Group,
> former President of Cartier International,
> President of EFMD (European Foundation for Management Development)
> and President of EDC (École des Dirigeants et Créateurs d'Entreprises)

To shape and express these goals, companies require charismatic leaders with vision. Strong captains need to provide direction to their teams, in order for the latter to navigate the boat, even in the strongest storm. The leaders need to set the rules, define the strategy and put in place a clear structure. No soccer team can become world champion without a strong captain to guide them to victory. Yet many brands have leaders with neither vision nor charisma. In such situations, role ambiguity prevails among teams.[4] Employees are uncertain about the management department's expectations and company goals. Salespeople, who are the ones supposed to row the boat, are usually among the first to be affected. Destabilization, demotivation and alienation from the brand are the consequences.

2.3   How to gain salespeople's trust

Heart-winner 8: Training! Training! Training!

> *Knowing more about a brand is like learning a new language. As soon as you start mastering the vocabulary, you are keen on talking.*
> (Shayda de Bary, Store Manager at Sonia Rykiel)

Regular training is one of the most important heart-winning strategies needed to retain salespeople in your company. In fact, training touches on all five of the emotional rings of sales force–brand relationships: love, identification, trust, pride and recognition.

The more a brand is willing to provide training sessions, the more a salesperson will be dedicated to the brand. Training is seen as the basic condition to selling. When professional, creative and regular training sessions are organized, the motivational effect increases. Brands that invest little in training will have real difficulty retaining their sales force, since a strong relationship between the sales force and the brand is unlikely to be established or maintained. Salespeople become demotivated if there is no or not enough training, and this leads to their disassociation with the brand over time.

---

[4] J. Singh and G. K. Rhoads (1997) "Boundary role ambiguity in marketing-oriented positions: a multidimensional, multifaceted operationalization." *Journal of Marketing Research*, 28, 328–38.

Having listened to so many salespeople and managers from various brands, I identified four main training categories: brand, product, sales technique and general culture, which can be implemented at various levels. Most brands combine parts of these four categories in each level of training.

The intensity of the training offered by a brand depends, of course, on the brand's size, its budget and the industry sector. In this chapter, I have provided a summary of the training tools that can be implemented in order to increase the trust salespeople have in the brand and thus reinforce sales force–brand relationships.

Brand training

This type of training should be provided when someone first joins the brand. It is designed to reveal the brand's strategy, its history, its values and vision. Training sessions are mostly led by brand trainers, together with product managers or marketing directors. In order to allow the new recruit to experience the brand's history, some brands organize these sessions in a location reminiscent of the brand's origins: the production site, for example, or the brand's own museum. In "Heart-winner 2," I listed numerous examples of brands that pass on the flame through a real and unique experience of the brand. Such experiences need to be designed in order to try and light a fire in the salespeople for the brand. This is only possible if the trainers are themselves passionate about the brand; they must embody it.

Product training

Product training is meant to ensure salespeople are experts on the products, so that they can feel competent when advising customers. Training in this area ranges from discovering the raw materials to the production process, to knowing customer benefits or understanding the actual range of the product. It is important to appeal to all senses and allow participants to test, touch, smell and try the products. If possible, the training sessions should be held where products are being made: in workshops or production sites. Allow new salespeople to get as close as possible to the product itself. The trainees must understand the value chain and see with their own eyes the complex and highly sophisticated processes that are required to obtain a final product that can be purchased. Salespeople understand why the brand has legitimacy by getting to know the product's technical aspects. They are then able to demonstrate why the product offers better solutions than the competition and justify its high price point.

> *I am convinced that I sell a credible product after attending highly technical trainings. Even if there is strong competition, I will feel confident arguing for my product since I don't have to lie or invent stories. We need to be able to trust a brand. If we don't trust it, we can't sell it.*
>
> (Dior sales associate)

If possible, have the experts themselves speak about their work: watchmakers, pearl farmers, doctors, researchers, jewelers and any kind of artists. Ideally, it is good to hold the training sessions where the experts work.

In order to train our teams before the launch of our new Abeille Royale product line, we invited a beekeeper to explain the secrets of the black bee of Ouessant, France. These bees produce a very special kind of honey, which is the main ingredient in the Abeille Royale line. The beekeeper explained his profession; each participant was automatically registered to become a member of the organization that protects this rare species. We also distributed honey made by these black bees. Instead of giving a PowerPoint presentation on the new product line, we set up an experiential and sensorial journey around the product: allowing participants to smell, touch, feel, taste and hear. Every stop in the journey was meant to teach them about a different aspect of the product line. This kind of training transmits both technical product knowledge and brand experience.

Such training is also very useful for illustrating the complex technologies used in our formulas. When we launched the third generation of our famous Orchidée Impériale skincare line, we developed an experiential method of training in order to help salespeople understand the concept of cell bioenergy. It is quite difficult to explain how the bioenergy of cells can be regenerated to a nonscientific person, such as a salesperson. So we decided to decorate the entire training room with special electric lamps,

> *allowing us to illustrate the scientific effect with the help of electric light.*
>
> (Agnès Combes, Training Director at Chanel,
> former International Training Director at Guerlain)

Louis Vuitton also identified the importance of touching and feeling as a key element in building salespeople's confidence and enthusiasm for new collections. It is the store manager's role to help salespeople discover the technical details that make the difference.

> *Every morning, I notice how the Louis Vuitton shop manager presents the new arrivals of the day to his sales team. Some 20 salespeople stand around him, while he explains the details of the products, then allows them to touch each product and discover its specificities. What he is actually doing is selling the products to his team before they sell it to their customers. He wants them to be fully confident. This ritual takes around 15 minutes. This starts the sales day with a new message, gives salespeople a specific focus and avoids routine. No other brand celebrates the morning briefing as well as Louis Vuitton.*
>
> (Alexandre Ferragu, former Retail Sales Manager Luxury &
> Accessories at Printemps)

In order to help salespeople remember all these technical product messages, training brochures and summaries are extremely helpful. The most detailed document is the brand-training book, which contains all the information about the product or brand. Summaries, however, provide product overviews that capture the most important messages. The quality and content of training tools show if the brand management really knows what is required in the field. A lot of feedback referring to inadequate training tools revealed the opposite: the focus is often on beautiful images, romantic words and inspirational design instead of providing pragmatic sales techniques, objectives and cross-selling strategies.

Sales technique training

Training dedicated to the art of selling should accompany brand and product training. In sales technique training sessions, salespeople should learn about the sales rituals that are specific to the brand, the vocabulary that needs to be used and the problems that may arise in difficult situations. These sessions are also meant to provide a better understanding of the industry sector, its competitors and customers. The content of this kind of training varies according to the salesperson's selling experience. It is therefore recommended to offer different types of training tools according to the level of expertise:

Level 1: Introduction to the art of selling
In the first year, each salesperson should attend a course to discover more about basic selling strategies and to get a general feel for the profession. If a brand is represented in a department store, such a sales environment becomes the perfect ground to learn. Young salespeople learn quickly what selling is all about in a business setting with high traffic, customer variety and overall speed.

Level 2: Advanced selling
In the second and third year, the more experienced salespeople should receive specific sales technique training, ideally provided by an external retail coach.

Level 3: Managing a team
In order to introduce a salesperson to basic management skills, it is advisable to provide him/her with a specific management training session, which should include topics such as management responsibilities and behavior.

Level 4: Managing a business unit
The most experienced salespeople, those who have shown excellent management skills, should then be trained to become store managers. The complexity of managing a business unit can be effectively taught through hands-on business games.

While company representatives should provide brand and product trainings, it is recommended that external trainers handle training sessions on sales techniques. This is because salespeople generally have a negative attitude toward management, feeling that representatives from the head offices have no idea what the sales jobs entail. External trainers bring along an objective vision, huge expertise and can provide examples from other brands in the relevant industry sector.

> *The external trainers chosen for our training sessions have coached sales-people from Rolex and IWC, and can say they have the same problems that we have. For over 20 years they have been training salespeople in the same sector, so they know what they are talking about.*
> (Arnaud Vidal, former Vice President Watches and Jewelry at Ralph Lauren and former General Manager of Audemars Piguet)

The best place to organize these sales technique trainings is in-store. That way, the sales environment is integrated in the entire ritual and salespeople can detect any methods/tools that need to be optimized in the store. Are products available? Are sales tables in the right place? Are they in the right format to optimize customer service? Is there anything blocking the salesperson from transforming the customer's desire into a sale?

Role play and sketches are among the most efficient training strategies in transmitting sales techniques. Since acting on stage and selling in the store have a lot in common, some companies decided to combine both worlds. In both situations, one needs to be convincing, dynamic, have a winning personality and be able to adapt in order to relate to the audience. Both salespeople and actors need to be able to play various roles according to each situation. They always need to be at their best.

Training in sales techniques that mix salespeople with performers are always highly appreciated.

> *Actors visited our stores as mystery shoppers and developed sketches based on their observations. During a great sales convention they performed these sketches, which were all so real. It was amazing! We, the salespeople, had to identify our mistakes and coach the performers on possible improve-ments. So they performed again, this time including our suggestions in order to improve the sales ritual. We had so much fun and learnt a lot.*
> (Fred sales associate)

> *For the launch of the fragrance Idylle, Guerlain asked me to develop a workshop in which I explained the sales ritual through dance. Every step in the sales process was translated into choreography I put together with choreographer Nathalie von Paris, to the song 'Singing in the Rain.' I started with welcoming the customer, showing them the movement,*

and everyone had to dance with me. When I met some of my participants two years later, they immediately recognized me as the dancer of Idylle.

(Raphael Rodriguez, professional dancer and coach)

General culture training

Besides being taught about the brand, its products and sales techniques, salespeople need to be prepared to work with a multitude of customers, their cultures, their issues and their behaviors. This is essential if you want your salespeople to trust your brand. Every day salespeople, especially those whose stores are situated in an international location, interact with a vast number of different characters and cultures.

Being familiar with someone else's culture creates sympathy, reduces barriers and encourages dialogue. Customers feel much more comfortable being served by salespeople who are familiar with their culture than by someone who has not made an effort to develop an understanding for it. Cultural competence increases sales. Brands that offer courses in intercultural management for specific cultures or allow salespeople to take language lessons are particularly well regarded by staff. Salespeople feel that their brand gives them the opportunity to learn something that will be useful in their role. They feel much better prepared when interacting with different customers and cultures.

> *Having the chance of learning about different cultures such as the Russians, the Chinese or the Japanese is highly interesting: we learn how they greet you, how we greet them, how to behave in the store in order to favor purchase. At the moment, I am learning Chinese in order to better serve our Chinese customers.*
>
> (Store manager at a high-end watchmaking brand)

It is important to encourage your sales teams to improve their general knowledge as well as preparing them to better understand intercultural differences. The best salespeople I met had an incredibly high amount of general knowledge, and one of their major preoccupations was related to maintaining this knowledge. When you interact with your customer on a high communication level, the customer feels understood and begins to trust you. It is only when customers trust their salespeople that they will open up and express their real needs, dreams and desires. It is therefore important to prepare your salespeople to discuss any kind of topic with the customer in order to capture the latter's attention.

Such cultural training shapes personalities, which is important when obtaining and maintaining a strong and convincing sales force.

Training is an extremely important way in which salespeople develop strong ties with their brand. However, training that ends up as a complete brainwash session can be very counterproductive. Such sessions suppress the salesperson's personality, which is regrettable since this is what makes the shopping experience unique for the customer. Salespeople should know all about products and techniques without having to change their personality. It is only by keeping the personal touch that they can be natural, credible and convincing.

The table below summarizes the four training categories every brand should consider when developing training sessions for salespeople.

Table 2   Training categories

	What?	Where?	Who?	How?	Why?
Brand Training	Brand history Values Strategies Vision	Head office Brand origin Brand museums	Brand trainer Marketing team General manager	Brand experience Top management presentation Meet the creator	Feel and understand the brand
Product Training	Raw materials Ingredients Research Production processes Product range	Production site Head Office	Product manager Production experts	Product discovery Sensorial experience Product trial Product manual	Experience the products Acquire product expertise Trust
Sales Technique Training	Level 1: Sales fundamentals Level 2: Specific sales techniques (objections, vocabulary, ritual, gestures, negotiation) Level 3: Team management Level 4: Store management	In store	Retail coaches External sales trainers Actors	Role-playing games Sketches	Dare to sell Transform Develop customer loyalty Recruit new customers
Cultural Training	Intercultural training Languages training	Intercultural management schools/ agencies	Intercultural management trainers Language teachers	Role-playing games Conversation	Dare to interact with the customer Interpret and understand the customer

It is necessary to adapt the nature of training sessions and their style throughout a salesperson's career (Figure 14).

1. Beginners are usually motivated since they are starting something new. However, their motivation needs to be structured and given a clear direction. When interacting with this section of the sales force, trainers should be guides, preparing trainees for the long path of success with the brand.

2. Advanced salespeople are in a different career phase. They have already encountered and sometimes even overcome the initial difficulties faced by new salespeople; they now ask themselves quite a lot of questions related to their profession and want to progress with more efficiency. They need to be accompanied by a coach, who adjusts rather than directs.

3. Highly experienced salespeople, who have been serving the brand for many years require a different type of training. They are proactive, autonomous and likely to become managers. It is therefore advised to provide them with management training led by external managers with high-level profiles. These trainers should then be respected thanks to their exceptional and diverse experience.

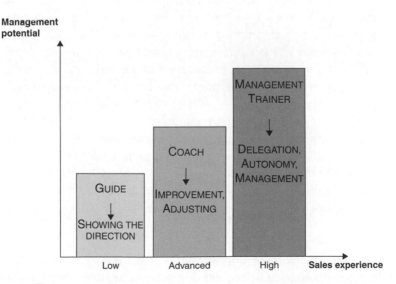

FIG 14 Trainer types for salespeople

Providing detailed, qualitative training for your sales force is essential in order to develop their relationship with your brand. Due to the importance of training, many brands have put in place special in-house training programs; some have even established their own schools or academies. At Chanel, for instance, salespeople are not active in the stores until they have gone through detailed training about the company culture, the products and sales techniques.

Van Cleef & Arpels built its own school, which is open to anyone who wants to learn more about the secrets of jewelry and high-end watchmaking. People from outside our company but also employees, including salespeople, can attend classes. The location of our school is extremely prestigious, as it is situated in a beautifully restored 18th-century building at Place Vendôme, the heart of the luxury jewelry and watchmaking industry. When salespeople attend these classes, they mix with others from different departments within the company as well as those with no link to it. They can even take classes with their clients. This widens the latter's understanding, giving them a deeper insight into our profession, and tightens customer–salesperson relationships. Since the sessions are extremely experiential, all participants have to become familiar with precious materials and techniques in order to produce an item. Don't you think a salesperson will talk differently about a piece of jewelry after having experienced the sophistication of the production process and the level of talent required to obtain the desired result? Besides, it will be easier for salespeople to explain the production process of a tailor-made masterpiece to a customer. The salesperson will be able to express the customer's wishes to the design studio much more clearly. In addition, he will be able to explain to the customer why certain special wishes take longer than expected or why they are very difficult to realize.

(Marie Vallanet-Delhom, President of the Van Cleef & Arpels School)

These observations make one wonder if it is necessary to train future salespeople thoroughly before allowing them to work for their respective brands. However, as the profession of sales associate does not have a highly prestigious reputation, business schools do not tend to offer sales diplomas. While the numbers of degrees available in marketing, finance or strategy are numerous, sales diplomas are extremely rare.

Heart-winner 9: Offer stability and structure!

Just as in a functioning relationship, strong and durable feelings build up over time between salespeople and the brand which they sell. Such feelings are a mixture of confidence, love and affection, shared moments and experiences. This might explain why I noticed particularly strong bonds between salespeople and their brands as brand seniority increased. For years, these salespeople live side by side with their brand. They share good and bad moments, successes and failures. They do everything to champion their brand and to transfer their passion to others, their customers.

However, a brand can only build a lasting, faithful and loving sales force if it offers stability from within. This begins with top management. When the president, CEO, general manager – or let's simply call him "captain" – changes frequently, the brand cannot expect to have the stability it needs to keep good staff. Brand relationships are built from the top. If the relationships are solid and sincere at the board level, they will trickle down to all levels in your company, reaching out to your sales force and customers. Stable brands have more loyal customers than brands that find their top management changing every two or three years. Change creates doubt, fear and rumors, which can lead to frustration and demotivation. Every change therefore needs to be conducted carefully and intelligently in order to avoid too much damage. Transparent communication and information are crucial.

> *Our general manager and president changed. Everything changed in our brand's organization. No more stability, no more structure. All the superiors with whom I used to work left. The new team does not know us or the values we bring to the brand. Our former president was extraordinary since he valued the importance of all sales teams in the field who fight for the brand's well-being every day. We are afraid that the new management won't have the same approach, won't recognize our work as much as he did.*
>
> (Store manager of a luxury fashion and accessory brand)

Providing stability and structure is important from a salesperson's first working day. This day is very important in a salesperson's career, since s/he gets his/her first impression. This moment can be compared to your first date with your potential husband/wife, whom you spotted on a dating website. The two of you have exchanged e-mails several times, felt a connection and decided to meet. You feel attracted to the person and this generates hope, but you are also scared, intimidated, feel insecure about the possible outcome. Many questions and emotions arise: Will I discover things I won't like, traits which are incompatible with my own values? Or will I fall in love at first sight? Was the picture s/he posted on the Internet a true image or did s/he modify his/her real face?

The relationship-building process between salespeople and brands starts on this very first day. Some brands put considerable effort into accompanying young salespeople throughout their integration process, which definitely pays off during the following collaboration period. In several countries, for instance, Guerlain delivers a manual called "My first 30 days at Guerlain" to their new salespeople, including all-important information needed at the beginning. A mentorship program has also been started in which senior staff members coach and initiate newcomers, sharing with them all-important best practices for a successful Guerlain career as a salesperson. Such measures help reinforce employee trust in the new brand and employer.

Stability can also be provided by setting certain structures or guidelines. Of course, I am not talking about a military regime with strict orders which don't leave space for personal interpretation. Rather, such guidelines are intended to show how the brand's inner values and convictions should be translated externally by those who are serving it. The degree of strictness varies from brand to brand. But it is important to indicate to the sales force how to appear, what to do and what not to do. This begins with their physical look, style and behavior.

> *We refunded hairdresser expenses since we wanted our salespeople to be impeccable, which is perfectly in line with Cartier's desire for excellence and attention to detail. At the same time, we expected them to wear cleaned and polished shoes. We had developed a guidebook on the*

Cartier salesperson's style in terms of makeup, nail lacquer, jewelry and, of course, dress-code.

(Nathalie Banessy Monasterio, former Retail Development Director at Richemont)

In sales especially, brand-specific and well-structured rituals help salespeople feel comfortable when fulfilling their selling "mission."

It is simply fantastic to work for a brand which offers a very unique shopping experience to our clients: the way we sell our products, how we welcome our clients, how salespeople work in their stores, the tools we have in order to tighten our relationships with our clients – everything is carefully thought through in detail.

(Louis Vuitton sales assistant)

The most unpleasant moments in a salesperson's life occur when clients are unsatisfied with their purchase, go back to the store and complain vehemently. Those who are directly confronted with these unhappy clients are the salespeople, even though the issue at stake is not usually their fault. Still, they are made responsible for product deficiencies since they are the people with whom clients relate. Brands that leave salespeople alone when they have to handle these touchy moments of customer interaction will lose their salespeople's trust. Brands therefore need to implement organizational structures that allow salespeople to feel supported during these destabilizing moments.

I worked in the high-end watchmaking and jewelry industry for six years and saw scenarios where a client took off his watch and threw it at the salesperson's face because it no longer worked. If a brand does not provide help in the form of a very professional and highly reactive after-sales service, the salesperson feels all alone when such verbal and even physical aggression happens.

(Nathalie Banessy Monasterio, former Retail Development Director at Richemont)

Brands must implement an initial-level rescue by ensuring their store managers are on hand to deal with the issue. They must be perfectly trained to handle any kind of objection or aggression. Since customer expectations are particularly high in the luxury industry, complaints are

ILL 8 / **The customer and his doctor**

(Source: Albert Dessinateur for Michaela Merk)

even more frequent and violent. Salespeople must therefore trust that their superior will be able to handle these situations with high professionalism. They need to be able to rely on them.

The next level is to establish an authentic after-sales service, even inside the store, in order to shorten the response/repair time. The more time you need to gain back customer satisfaction, the higher the negative word-of-mouth effect. Don't give angry clients a chance to carry their annoyance beyond your doorstep! Catch the problem as early as possible and avoid its escalation. To do so requires in-depth after-sales training, efficient after-sales structures and a professional after-sales attitude. One of the key attitudes that brands need to integrate and communicate is honesty! Nobody's perfect, even in luxury. Be transparent with your salespeople and clients about possible technical problems, quality issues and product deficiencies and make a sincere effort to solve them. Honesty pays!

If a €10,000 watch no longer works, our demanding customers get angry. They have trouble understanding why such highly expensive watches might stop ticking after a while. This is the moment when I intervene. As our store's after-sales manager, my role is essential every day, since watches need to be revised, just like cars. Our salespeople feel secure because they have an expert on the spot who will treat these issues and calm down angry clients. My role is to solve problems, reassure clients and our salespeople. I am like a doctor who accompanies patients until they are cured again. It is not a salesperson's job to do this, since after-sales service is a different profession and requires very specific knowledge and a particular attitude. You need to be extremely humble and empathetic in order to identify the real problem, show understanding for the problem and fix it. However, I train salespeople to handle the first contact with the unhappy clients before they hand over the case to me.

(Assistant store manager and after-sales services manager at a
high-end watchmaking brand)

Trusting relationships between salespeople and brands can also be fostered if healthy reporting systems are put in place. These systems generate exchange and transparency, and allow salespeople to inform superiors of any deficiencies. They should not give the impression of serving as accusation tools in order to potentially denounce salespeople who make mistakes. They should instead be perceived as a chance to share observations, ideas, possible improvements and results with management. If practiced in the right spirit, reporting systems are very efficient tools that build trust and favor communication.

Every Saturday evening, our stores send their weekly report, which can be both qualitative and quantitative. They can write as much about the weather as the number of newly recruited clients, their profile, or the products they sold during the week. At the end of the season we also ask them to put together a summary and tell us more about the positive aspects and improvements that could be made. The yearly 360-degree interviews are equally important. They allow both managers and salespeople to draw a picture of the past year. We also ask them to

self-evaluate before these interviews. This allows us to see how they see themselves. Then we confront our vision. With this process, we generate high transparency and salespeople increasingly trust us and the brand.
(Elodie Leprince-Ringuet, International Retail Director at Robert Clegerie, former European Retail Director at Bonpoint)

Heart-winner 10: Don't put them in chains!

It's only when salespeople feel trusted by their managers that they are able to develop trust in their brand. This is a mutual process, which takes some time to establish and grow. Within this manager–sales force–trust model, we can distinguish two different types of trust:

1 – Trust in professional capabilities and talents

This form of trust finds its expression in two different behavior patterns:

a) When managers grant early responsibilities to salespeople and allow them to climb the career ladder.

ILL 9 / The manager and his prisoners

(Source: Albert Dessinateur for Michaela Merk)

In my sales force interviews it became evident that salespeople developed close relationships with their brand if they were offered unexpected career opportunities. This could include, for example, an appointment to a position higher than their officially acquired skills seem to merit.

> *My relationship with Fendi definitely rests on mutual trust. Not quite one year after my arrival I was offered the chance of managing a store even though I had never worked in retail before. The opportunity came when my superior left the company. Their decision to put me in this position at such an early stage of my career was an incredible sign that they trusted my abilities. They gave me an amazing opportunity, so I started trusting in them. It's true: today we move ahead hand in hand.*
>
> (Fendi store manager)

> *They recruited me as after-sales manager and soon after they promoted me to the assistant store manager position. They identified my talent and passion for high-end watches and for the brand.*
>
> (Assistant store manager and after-sales services manager at a high-end watchmaking brand)

b) When managers allocate salespeople a certain degree of freedom to act.

If managers put salespeople in chains, if they control closely each step they take, salespeople will feel pressured and not trusted. The more salespeople gain seniority and experience within their profession, the more it is important to give them some freedom to act. This affects all areas: store management, merchandising, order and stock management, sales force training and local event organization. This does not mean that you should not provide your stores with guidelines, corporate measures or information and structure. However, a certain degree of local input puts salespeople in a different position. They feel taken seriously, respected, trusted, needed, important and useful. Consequently, they will be more responsible for their actions. If you don't make your employees feel responsible, you won't make them go that extra mile and, even worse, they won't put any extra effort into their work. An example of such freedom would be allowing your stores to take some initiatives on a local basis without them having to ask the head office for approval, and allocating budgets to your sales teams for these kinds of activities.

> *In order to be reactive in the field, it's a big advantage to be allowed to take local initiatives without having to obtain the approval of superiors. Whenever I want to organize a cocktail for my clients, I create my own invitation visuals and mailings and decide whom to invite. Since we are much closer to our clients than our managers in the head office, we can target our actions much more appropriately.*
>
> (Fendi sales associate)

Salespeople feel free when brands respect their personalities and their own selling rituals. The same brand philosophy and selling method can be expressed differently according to the person who does the selling. This is what makes a brand spicy, interesting and human. All salespeople are different in character. It's only when they can be themselves that they can overperform and relate to the brand.

> *You should not force them to say things or behave against their own nature and personality. What is important is that they get the core message of the brand and interpret it.*
>
> (Michel Guten, Sup de Luxe President, Vice President Comité Champs-Élysées, former Vice President of Cartier)

2 – Trust in salespeople–customer relationships

This is a golden rule to respect: sales managers should never interfere in salespeople's ties with their clients. These relationships have been carefully established over time and are among the most precious elements a brand can own. They are built on mutual feelings of trust and confidence between the salesperson and the customer. Even if a customer is a highly respected public personality, the manager should not interfere. Doing so could, in the worst-case scenario, even lead to an immediate breakup between the salesperson and the brand s/he serves.

> *As a manager it is important not to interfere in the relationships salespeople have with their customers, since these ties are very personal. Whenever stars, famous actors or politicians entered*

our boutiques, it would have been a big mistake to meet them, even if you are the brand's general manager. These people come to the store to see their favorite salesperson, whom they trust and know personally. You should even avoid to be seen in the store. Discretion is essential in our business. Well-known customers don't like others to know where they are. They don't appreciate it if the brand management team learns of their presence. You need to be able to distance yourself, take a step back – this is luxury. I remember one day when Mr. Sarkozy entered our flagship store. It was just unthinkable for anyone in top management to go to the boutique downstairs to welcome him personally.

(Christian Blanckaert, Professor in Luxury Management at ESCP Europe and former CEO of Hermès Sellier and Hermès International)

In order to help salespeople reinforce their customer relationships, some brands even allow their best salespeople to use credit cards in order to invite their most prestigious clients for lunch or dinner. They do not even have to call their superior for approval. All they have to do is hand in the invoice to head office. This is a privilege that is not given to most top managers working at head office. These kinds of business practices are

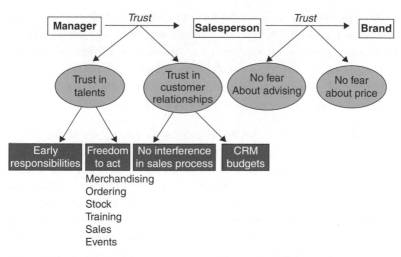

FIG 15 / The Manager–Salesperson–Brand (MSB) chain of trust

important relationship-building tools for the type of salesperson who has been able to sell a €50,000 watch to one of his/her trusted clients.

> *Top managers should do everything possible in order to foster sales force–customer relationships. Along with our best clients I was invited to attend the last dinner at the famous restaurant El Bulli in Barcelona before it closed. I had never been to this legendary place before and was very keen to go. However, I decided to allow my best salesperson to go. I did not go myself since I felt there would be a certain incoherence: it was the task of the person who had established the customer contact to attend the event.*
> (Arnaud Vidal, former Vice President Watches and Jewelry at Ralph Lauren and former General Manager of Audemars Piguet)

Heart-winner 11: Share what you can!

Salespeople's hearts can be broken if you don't communicate enough or leave them feeling uncertain about their role and/or performance. This is particularly true in times of economic downturns and difficult periods for your brand, such as brand takeovers or new top management. Every change includes an element of fear, even among the most experienced salespeople. Brands that have previously managed to build strong relationships over time can see their ties break if they don't master the communication required in these situations.

Many companies make the mistake of not communicating at all with their lower-level staff, in order to retain information. Yet silence breaks relationships and previously established trust. It generates stress and rumors, which are usually worse than reality. Top management obviously need to evaluate the type of content they can share with their teams. But retaining information is one of the worst strategic decisions.

> *Many changes are currently happening within our brand but we are left without any information. During the last sales seminar, which was meant to be fun and foster team spirit, no one could enjoy it. Everyone just wanted to finish dinner and go to bed even though we were in an amazing location. What a pity! It was so counterproductive. I believe that if top management had explained the situation to us, even if it was negative and difficult for the brand, we could have understood. It would have been crucial to inform us sufficiently before the seminar, to provide us with facts, instead of organizing the event as*

ILL 10 The manager sharing with his disciples

(Source: Albert Dessinateur for Michaela Merk)

if everything was under control. Now we are all about to go on holiday and still don't know what will happen to us in September, once we are all back.

(Sales representative of a selective beauty brand)

In times when companies are bought by investment funds and undergo frequent changes in proprietorship, employees tend to lose their trust in their employer. Change is always scary; this is human. That is why it is so important to reinforce our strategic positioning, direction and values. If you share these clearly with your teams, they will feel reassured. Considerable pedagogical effort is required to explain where you want to go. I believe many companies often underestimate the importance of sharing the vision with the sales force, of making sure that they also understand it. Just as we communicate our direction to investors, we must also communicate our convictions to our own salespeople to gain their trust and maintain stability. They are our ambassadors. They represent our house.

(Elodie Leprince-Ringuet, International Retail Director at Robert Clergerie, former European Retail Director at Bonpoint)

2.4   How to make salespeople feel proud of your brand

Heart-winner 12: Let your brand shine beyond your stores!

What makes salespeople talk about their brand outside their working environment when interacting with their friends and families? It is a strong feeling of pride! Pride for their brand and its products. Brand managers should regularly ask themselves what they could change about their brand in order to make their sales force feel proud of serving the brand from morning to evening.

Over the course of my interviews, I saw that brands were doing particularly well in this area if they managed to develop products as if they were iconic stars, which would thus have a big impact even beyond the stores. This entire process is in line with systematic efforts made to build strong brand awareness among potential customers. As soon as

ILL 11 / Strong brands shine beyond your stores!

(Source: Albert Dessinateur for Michaela Merk)

the brand name is mentioned, it should ring a bell, since this popularity makes salespeople proud.

> *I have always chosen to work for brands that carry a famous and magic name. Today, I am so incredibly proud of working for the extraordinary brand Dior. Seeing a three-minute campaign about a new Dior fragrance is true enjoyment for me. The brand's omnipresence is simply exceptional. It is just like during the fashion show period. You can't imagine how proud we are when the new collections are publicly revealed. Then I tell myself how lucky I am to serve such a great brand. Fashion shows make journalists, clients but also us, the salespeople, dream.*
>
> (Dior shop assistant)

Fashion shows represent the moment when the press, VIPs, experts, employees and the public get to see the upcoming season's new styles, the inspiration of their genius creators, the trends to come. Such shows reinforce people's bonds with your brand more than any other event during the year.

> *Those who have worked for Prada know that you are simply filled with pride whenever Prada presents its new collection. Everyone is thrilled. Amazing, this is Prada! The brand directors attended the event. We followed the show in the boutique on our iPhones or on TV at home in the evening. The following day, we were all so enthusiastic, which could immediately be seen through the sales figures. We were commenting on the looks we had discovered and exchanging our first impressions on what we were going to sell. So exciting! Fashion shows are extremely important for brands. After the show, all company members feel so concerned about the given message. However, it would have been even better if a screen had been set up in-store for everyone to follow the show live and then go out and celebrate together.*
>
> (Former Store Manager at Prada)

As well as being a wonderful arena in which to reveal new products, fashion shows are also the perfect place to highlight the new collection's creator. Talent is made public, anchored stars confirm their loyalty and allow the brand to have a presence beyond the stores:

> *Mrs. Prada lets the brand shine through her collections and advertising campaigns that fill all who work for her with pride. This pride makes them talk to their families and friends about Mrs. Prada's creations; they make the brand shine wherever they go. They carry a piece of her glory inside themselves.*
>
> (Natalie Bader, CEO of Prada France,
> former President at Fred International, former Marketing Director at Sephora)

One must understand the brand perfectly to feel pride for it. Once again, we come back to the importance of training, which allows salespeople to understand and embody the brand. This is the foundation on which to build a sales force that is proud of its brand.

Tools that help positively reinforce brand awareness among customers in a positive way generate pride and strengthen sales force–brand relationships. This branding process starts with the development of a strong iconic logo, which can be recognized across cultures. Several luxury brands have done an amazing job in creating logos, which can be recognized just by their symbol: Rolex has its crown, Mercedes its star, Lacoste its crocodile; these are prefect examples of strong branding through the logo.

Striking, easily recognizable logos as well as iconic products help generate pride among salespeople. Customers should be able to associate a brand name and a product design simply by hearing the name of the product. Brands that manage to bring a specific product design to global fame have a good chance of stimulating salespeople's pride, such as Hermès with its legendary Kelly Bag, Louis Vuitton with its Monogram Bag or Audemars Piguet with its famous "montre octogonale." The brand's former CEO, Arnaud Vidal, explains:

> *One day a 72-year-old designer developed a watch with eight angles. It became the brand's emblem and represents around 80 percent of our sales today. This iconic product transformed Audemars Piguet from being highly traditional to being a modern and successful brand, making those who wear it and sell it proud.*

In 1967 we created our leading model Alhambra, which was inspired by the stained glass windows of the Alhambra Palace in Grenada, Spain. It had this beautiful Arabic touch. While it was quite popular after its creation, this pattern somehow fell into oblivion until a few years ago. This is when we gave the Alhambra model a revival with the vintage model. This revival was a key aspect of the house's success today. Women love them. Even young girls ask their grandmothers to give them their old Alhambra chains since they are crazy about them. The amazing popularity of the house's strong iconic symbol made us produce them in all lengths, colors, types, as necklaces, earrings etc. This tremendous success is comparable to Cartier's three rings, which were ordered by the French poet Jean Cocteau in 1924 and are now one of the most emblematic gifts parents can give their daughter on her 18th birthday.

(Brigitte Smadja, Van Cleef & Arpels Store Manager)

When a salesperson sells such iconic products in stores that are located in prestigious places related to glamour, high society and pure luxury, they literally feel in heaven. They feel particularly proud if they can tell their friends that they work in Paris, Place Vendôme, Avenue Montaigne or in New York, Madison Avenue. Of course, brands can often use this to compensate their best performing salespeople: by allowing them to serve in the most beautiful flagship stores. It is interesting to observe how much the store location influences the salesperson's pride in the brand. The greatest feeling of pride in the brand can usually be found among salespeople who work in these emblematic locations. They tend to be the strongest brand ambassadors and models for other salespeople. Their pride in the brand should spill over to the entire sales force, and this can be facilitated by organizing integration periods for salespeople through team meetings, or by letting new employees spend time in a flagship store at the beginning of their career. They need to experience the pride of belonging to a strong brand before leaving the epicenter.

Brands can also make an impact beyond their stores by developing striking advertising campaigns in which the brand DNA is communicated to the world. The more a brand is exposed externally, the more it is celebrated, and the more the salesperson feels proud of working for such an iconic brand.

> *When Cartier launched the film L'Odyssée, it generated a mind-blowing wave of pride among salespeople from all over the world. It managed to reinforce their link with the brand since the film got such positive feedback from the press, VIPs, retailers and clients. All these compliments were not just appreciated by top management and the communication department but by all employees. I remember, when we viewed the film for the first time in the stores, the teams were stunned. It generated an amazing 'wow effect' and during the following weeks everyone was so enthusiastic that it immediately translated into the sales figures. True commitment and pride could be felt among all teams around the world thanks to the film.*
>
> (Nathalie Banessy Monasterio, former Retail Development Director at Richemont)

It is widely known that advertisements which use famous international faces help brands gain global recognition. While this marketing strategy of star endorsement reinforces customers' identification with their beloved brand, it has a particularly strong effect on salespeople's feeling of pride for the brand. Salespeople have the privilege of serving customers in the name of a star. In addition, they pursue the same goal as the star: to be the brand's ambassadors.

> *Today, Julia Roberts gives our brand worldwide impact. She is one of our brand's key ambassadors. Everyone knows her. Lancôme is fully associated with Julia Roberts; actually, the brand is Julia Roberts. Then we have another strong symbol: the rose. Other brands often envy us for being represented by this beautiful flower, which has a lot of meaning, and many copy us. The rose is the most universally recognized and majestic flower, standing for femininity, elegance and authenticity.*
>
> (Sandrine Sabathé, Sales Representative at Lancôme)

The most exciting moment in a salesperson's life is when they, as ambassadors, get to meet other ambassadors. Brands should, therefore, not only display their stars on screen but promote encounters between the stars and their own sales force, for instance in flagship stores.

> *When we organized the encounter between our brand ambassador Andy Roddick and the sales teams in New York for the store opening on Fifth Avenue, the effect was incredibly strong. The sales team followed all of his tennis matches and sent tweets to their colleagues to support Andy. All this because they had the unique chance of meeting a megastar who embodied their brand.*
>
> (Alexandre Fauvet, former Executive Vice President at Lacoste)

Besides the original creators, the most important brand ambassadors are the top managers. They travel all over the world to spread the brand's message to local teams. Some of them are true media stars who give interviews in the press and are seen as highly influential business personalities. Salespeople perceive their president's visit – especially when they are true media figures – as a high honor.

> *One week before my store visit in Berlin I opened a new shop in China. The pictures of this opening ceremony were published in the press and sent to all of our stores. When I then came to Berlin, the sales team felt so proud to receive their brand president, who had just been in China a week ago and was now in Germany to spend time with them. This was an eye-opener for me, to see the impact of such international media coverage on our own teams.*
>
> (Elisabeth Cazorla, President of Jacadi)

In addition, brands that are market leaders or that experience a huge popularity surge tend to generate enormous pride among their employees. Most brands with strong positive brand awareness also benefit from comfortable positions in the marketplace. Besides positive sellout figures compared to competitors, brands that are in a leadership position also make salespeople feel extremely privileged in being chosen to sell a leader's products. They are among the best who sell the best.

Below, I want to sum up the six most important facets in the marketing mix that allow brands to successfully undertake the "walk of fame," and fill their salespeople with enormous pride (Figure 16).

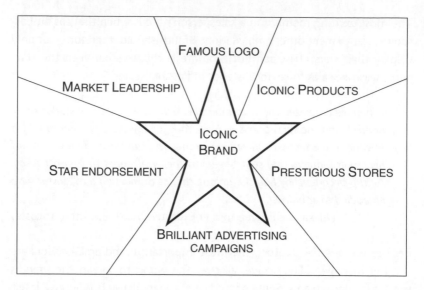

FIG 16 The marketing mix of fame

Heart-winner 13: No limits to quality, innovation and creativity!

High quality and product excellence are the basis for customer and sales force loyalty. It should be the utmost goal for every brand to generate not only trust but also pride in the brand! Salespeople should feel it is a privilege to sell their brand's treasures.

Intense training processes are needed to transmit pride about product quality. Videos of sophisticated production processes or direct visits to production sites are very useful. Salespeople need to understand how their products exceed their competitors' in quality. Salespeople should even have a certain healthy feeling of superiority without becoming arrogant. Why not allow your experts to talk about their profession? They could share their pride in the products, in the production processes, and share the secrets surrounding the product's creation with their own sales force.

Conversely, a lack of quality has been revealed to be the most radical heartbreaker. My research among more than 400 salespeople showed how quality deficiencies could negatively impact salespeople's relationships with their brands, leading to abrupt breakups between the two. Quality can be related to the product itself but also to the person representing it. If brand representatives prove to be incompetent, no lasting relationship can be established. They play a key role in transmitting trust and pride. The numerous Sephora and Marionnaud sales associates I interviewed during the course of my PhD research confirmed that the role of the brand representatives was extremely important. If they are not sympathetic or competent, this impacts salespeople's relationships with the brand and their motivation to sell it. Many brands underestimate the importance of their representatives. If they don't prove to be experts in their field, especially in front of highly experienced senior salespeople, the impact on the latter's relationship with the brand can be very negative. A high turnover of brand representatives can also cause serious damage in the mutual relationship with the sales force. But the worst damage is done when brands don't send anyone to promote or explain the products to the sales force. Consequently, sales associates who work for multi-brand retailers have difficulty establishing any kind of relationship with these brands – and this directly translates into lower sales figures.

Pride in your brand can also be related to the brand's origin. When it comes to manufacturing, so many production processes have been outsourced to low-cost markets, that producing in Europe brings a certain degree of prestige. However, if luxury brands switch from "made in Italy" or "made in France" to "made in China," the deception can be wide-ranging, both among customers and salespeople.

Besides excellent quality, brands can encourage bonds with their sales-people through creativity and innovation. The sense of pride in the salespeople of an Apple store is almost tangible when you enter. They are keen to demonstrate what they know and what their technology can do. Their brand, its creator and the entire innovative technology around it has transformed them into trendsetters. On a daily basis, they show customers how to make life easier by using digital tools, or make them feel they're cool if they own a new Mac device. This pride is even demon-strated to the outside world through Apple's transparent storefronts. Everyone can see the impact of modernity and innovation, which are part of the brand, even outside of the store.

In high-end watchmaking, innovation is a key aspect that bonds sales-people to the brand. Watches are expected to be reliable companions, sophisticated, precise and a product of excellence. Some brands can look back at a long history of innovations and creations, which makes their brand president and their sales force extremely proud:

> *Innovation is what makes our brand so exclusive and unique since its creation in 1780, when Breguet invented and commercialized the first automatic watch. Simply by wearing it, it moved. We also invented new ways of wearing watches. The first watch that was worn around the wrist was produced by Breguet in 1810 for Caroline Bonaparte, the younger sister of Napoleon I of France. Before that, everyone had pocket watches on chains or ribbons. They were regarded as very intimate objects and never shown publicly. This innovation was so progressive, however, that it took a long time to really establish wristwatches in society. Still today, we deposit around ten patents every year. Our salespeople are very proud of working for a brand that embodies innovation every day.*
>
> (Emmanuel Breguet, Brand Manager of Breguet France and in charge of the brand's heritage)

Some fashion brands, such as Prada, are extremely good at innovating and setting new styles.

This is one of the reasons why Prada salespeople whom I interviewed, as compared to salespeople for other brands, expressed the most pride in their brand and in the extraordinary talent of its creators.

> *Miuccia Prada is a genius. She is incredible. She can't be described. She is surprising. She is 3km ahead of all other products on the market. You can recognize the fruit of infinite reflection that leads to perfection. This woman thinks a lot before she creates. Nothing is launched if it is not 100 percent approved, finalized and ready to market.*
>
> (Former Store Manager at Miu Miu)

Other brands innovate not only through new technology but also by introducing new forms of service, styles or colors, always adapting to changing taste in our society. By innovating they help people feel better, live better, be happier. At the same time, salespeople are proud to sell products that bring joy to their customers. They become "happymakers."

Alain Nemarq, President of Mauboussin, shared with me his vision of innovation:

> *While jewelry needed to be minimalistic in the past, it will need to be extravagant tomorrow for two reasons: first of all because jewelry is a way to exist, since it allows you to be seen, to stand out. Second, jewelry serves to protect you. Jewelry is like a second skin that has this important double function in our world where it has become so difficult to be someone and where dangers are omnipresent. A beautiful necklace can add some color to people's lives, now that lives have become so grey and sad since the crisis started dominating Europe. So our salespeople feel proud to help clients find their secret weapons to survive tomorrow. Extreme creativity, originality and excellence are the key elements we need to communicate throughout our masterpieces.*

Innovations trigger dynamism, animation, action and change; all of which are felt in the boutique between salespeople and customers. This reinforces the link salespeople have with their brands. Innovation fosters dynamism and enthusiasm among teams. This is what drives your business. Without innovation, salespeople get bored, lose the connection with the brand and quit.

Heart-winner 14: Communicate your achievements!

How can your teams be proud of your brand if they don't even know what is going on with it? Communication at all levels within your company is essential in order to stimulate awareness, knowledge and pride. Inform them about your brand and your corporation's minor and major victories, if the brand is embedded in a bigger company structure. Throughout my interviews I realized that salespeople had a strong desire to be better informed. I also noticed that little was done to give them positive information that

ILL 12 / We are the best!

(Source: Albert Dessinateur for Michaela Merk)

went beyond communication around targets and figures. I heard multiple excuses: "We don't have the time to prepare and transmit the information," "We should do it, but never put it in place," "We haven't even thought about it," "They should focus on their selling tasks rather than this."

What kind of information would be particularly useful to pass on to sales-people in order to arouse their pride in the brand?

- The positive rankings of your products, or your brand versus the competition on a global scale.
- Awards for creative merchandising, product development, advertising campaigns.
- Information about your brand's international expansion including store openings.
- Product launches before they become public.
- New advertising campaigns before they air on TV.

- Big events such as fashion shows or VIP events to share the new collection.
- Best-practice activities in your stores around the world.
- Honors for particular achievements.
- Articles in the press that mention your brand.
- TV shows about your industry, citing your brand.
- Public interviews of the brand's top management or the brand creator.

Depending on your field, this list can be indefinitely extended.

There are multiple occasions and communication tools in and with which to spread motivating messages; internal newsletters and the intranet network are very efficient channels of information that reach each team member instantaneously and on a regular basis.

Events such as team gatherings and seminars are great occasions in which to communicate positive messages to your salespeople in a stronger way. Make them feel part of the achievements of the brand, since each team member can help make the brand grow. Show them to what extent their personal input contributed to a great outcome.

During our retail seminars we present the latest achievements to our management teams, such as an exhibit in New York or Prada's most recent epicenter store openings in Rodeo Drive, Tokyo and New York. We inform them about our foundation, about all activities related to art and the latest success stories from our fashion shows. These messages are then passed on by our managers to all sales teams. We need to fuel them so that they can tell our success stories to their customers. In addition, our press department puts all the press appearances together to produce a little magazine that is sent every week to all our stores and our company restaurant. This is where people can have a look at the week's press articles and always be perfectly informed. For instance, if a customer asks about a red dress she has seen in ELLE magazine, the salesperson knows what article she is referring to.

(Natalie Bader, CEO of Prada France, former President at Fred International, former Marketing Director at Sephora)

It is no secret that people who obtain honors and victories feel proud of their accomplishments, but this also generates pride among their friends, associates, team members or their community. In order to acknowledge merit, each competition has its own symbol, or logo, a reward that is handed over to the best. I believe that challenges stimulate business in a positive sense and make us more competitive. This is why I created the European Beauty Innovation Awards for young high-end beauty brands from across the world. The prize is negotiation opportunities with the top management of leading cosmetics retailers in Europe. Each winning brand is allowed to use the logo of the awards on its products and in the press. It is very difficult for young brands to get their breakthrough. It is also particularly difficult to find salespeople who want to work for young brands at a stage when they are still unknown. One of the best indirect effects these awards have is that these young brands generate pride for their brand and the team that made the victory possible. Elodie Pollet, the brand creator of the selective fragrance brand Eutopie and winner of the European Beauty Innovation Awards 2012, told me with pride:

> These awards were a unique opportunity for my young fragrance brand Eutopie to be seen by top retailers all across Europe. It was amazing to get a chance to present my brand to CEOs and purchasing directors during the competition. They liked it and I won the opportunity of negotiating with almost all retailers. Today, thanks to the European Beauty Innovation Awards, Eutopie is listed in very prestigious stores in Germany, Switzerland and Austria. For my brand, it was a very efficient, market-driven, beneficial contest in every aspect.

Once a brand is listed in a retailer's portfolio you need to find salespeople. But who wants to work for a no-name? Awards like these help young brands acquire status, visibility and popularity. These brands become stars overnight, making things much easier with regard to sales.

Award-winning logos and honors can be put on products but also on clothes and uniforms. These permanently remind your team of the brand's excellence. The sister of Patrick Roger, famous award-winning chocolate designer and founder of his own brand, commented:

My brother always wears his blue, white and red uniform which stands for the MOF title (Meilleurs Ouvriers de France = the best manufacturers of France). Every four years, the French government honors artisans with special talents in craftsmanship, such as innovation, technical skills, respect for tradition and refinement. It is very difficult to obtain this title, which you keep for your lifetime. The entire team is so proud that Patrick was chosen for this title in the name of our brand. In our boutiques we talk about this title and the Japanese customers are really crazy about it. Being honored means a lot in their culture.

In a sales context particularly, where management must motivate large, sometimes geographically remote, teams, the communication flow needs to be carefully structured. Regular conference calls between retail managers and their sales force are great opportunities to share achievements and ensure the latter feel proud of their contributions. And, on every store level, the daily morning briefing should also be used as a unique moment to share the brand's small and big victories.

Along with our weekly store manager meetings, we have put in place an online communication tool. This is a perfect platform to share brand and human victories, such as promotions and awards.

(Elisabeth Cazorla, President of Jacadi)

Information that concerns our company and that is not confidential is immediately communicated to our teams. For instance, we organize a number of events in our stores, which are photographed; the images and information are later shared with everyone in our company via regular newsletters. This is very important, not only to inform but also to give the teams the impression of being involved and connected on a daily basis. This information flow should include facts and figures but also emotional encouragement. They should be fun to read and nice to look at.

(Elodie Leprince-Ringuet, International Retail Director at Robert Clergerie, former Bonpoint European Retail Director)

Elodie Leprince-Ringuet told me that pride was also generated through informing the sales force about press articles related to the brand. For instance, in an interview for *ELLE* magazine, a famous fashion designer recently praised one of Bonpoint's salespeople at Avenue Montaigne as one of the best sales associates in the world. Since she was mentioned by her first name, it was easy to identify her. This is why Elodie Le Prince-Ringuet decided to send her a message of congratulation, as did many other colleagues. This attention from the general manager generated so much pride among the entire team.

Another example she gave me was when Michelle Obama came to Bonpoint's flagship store in Paris:

> *All the press articles about this unique event were collected and shared within our corporation.*

All these examples illustrate how sharing communication and information about brand highlights can have a positive impact on employees' feeling of pride and identification.

2.5   How to enhance your sales force's brand recognition

Heart-winner 15: Enrich your brand's service level!

Of all the factors that influence sales force recognition, customers have the strongest impact. Brands need to develop tools and strategies that encourage customers to express their satisfaction toward sales teams. This usually happens when their expectations are exceeded, when the service they have received has been better than average, when they were surprised about special attention, when salespeople managed to anticipate their customers' desires.

It is impressive to see how greatly customers can influence the well-being of salespeople in their profession. Salespeople are thrilled when they make their clients happy. They are even more excited when clients express their happiness and decide to come back again. Happy clients make happy salespeople.

> *The most incredible recognition we can get from our customers are thank-you letters for excellent service. Sometimes they also give us a call*

ILL 13 / Customer service sense

(Source: Albert Dessinateur for Michaela Merk)

after their visit in our store. This is priceless and encourages us to provide even better support next time.

(Assistant store manager and after-sales services manager
at a high-end watchmaking brand)

Most brands and companies focus on developing their customer loyalty potential in order to gain a huge customer base and profile their customers for targeted marketing actions. However, they rarely consider the positive secondary effect this has on their sales force: when brands provide products and services that make customers want to return on a regular basis, the sales force's loyalty to its employer is strengthened (see Figure 17). On the one hand, this can be explained by the fact that salespeople get more recognition for their expertise and advice from their customers during the sales process. On the other hand, salespeople perceive service and loyalty potential as precious brand support. They feel secure working for a brand where their efforts in advising and selling pay off in the long run.

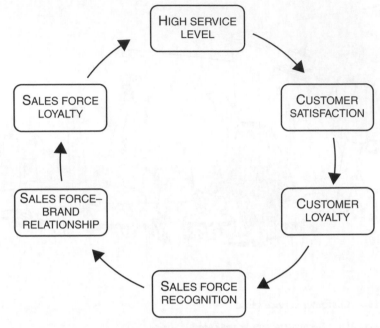

FIG 17 / The customer–sales force–loyalty cycle

When brands develop products and services that allow salespeople to strengthen customer loyalty, the sales force binding potential increases. This becomes clear when analyzing statements made by sales associates in the watch and jewelry industry:

> It is great that our brand has put so much effort in developing the bridal branch. This allows us to follow our clients first as young couples, then throughout the all-important stages in their lives. First you advise the future couple in their choice of engagement rings. The wedding follows a few months later. Seeing the couple come back to me and chose their wedding ring from my brand is the highest form of recognition. A year later comes the baby, so I express my congratulations with a nice hand-written card. Having established a relationship of trust, the couple usually comes back again to choose the necklace for their child's baptism, and so on. If a brand, like ours, has developed beautiful products with which to serve clients in all-important stages in life, customers provide the most amazing and emotional testimonials for the salespeople who served them.
>
> (Fred sales associate)

Customer service can also be provided by offering high-level expertise in the stores or by incorporating areas, which are exclusively dedicated to brand experience and not necessarily to sales transactions.

> *On the first floor of our flagship boutique on Place Vendôme we built a museum about Breguet's history in watchmaking. This space is not commercial at all; there are no logos and no prices. Salespeople love taking customers upstairs to give them more information about the brand and to build trust. In this space, salespeople feel valued since they are the experts and guides. In addition, we offer a very special service to our customers who bring along old watches and want to know when the watch was designed. Unfortunately, we are forced to tell many customers that their watch is actually not a real antique. This occurs frequently with models that date from the 19th century. In order to find out if the watch is real or a copy, we have to find out the date of the model, which is listed in our archive books.*
>
> (Emmanuel Breguet, Brand Manager of Breguet France
> and in charge of the brand's heritage)

Recognition expressed by customers is crucial for sales force satisfaction. But recognition coming from colleagues and superiors within the company should also be developed. What would help is to change the way the different services interact with each other, since all services are each other's clients: salespeople are the clients of the training department, the training department is the product development department's client and the product development department is the research unit's client. This kind of internal service company spirit requires everyone to offer the best possible service from within and strengthen associate brand loyalty.

Heart-winner 16: Be close to the field!

In many companies, salespeople feel like they are least listened to out of all employees. They feel that their reality in the field is far away from the head office's reality, where all decisions are taken. Salespeople are even convinced that managers don't dare to come and see them in order to avoid discovering the toughness of day-to-day business, the less shiny realities of the brand, and the difficulties of dealing with the unsatisfied and highly demanding customer. This impression silences the voice of many salespeople; they virtually stop sharing their ideas and observations with those above them.

As soon as someone from top management shows some interest in their activities, salespeople are astonished, surprised, can hardly believe what is happening. In many companies, since the motivation to share was lost a long time ago, managers don't expect to hear about salespeople's field experiences any more. In numerous cases, too, salespeople don't dare speak up. They fear that the reality they pass on would destroy the brand illusion, would make them become negative messengers and would accelerate their dismissal. Deep inside, they believe that no one wants to listen to their opinion anyway, since they are simply salespeople. Therefore, it is important for managers to clearly signal to the sales force that their views are important.

So what should managers do in order to achieve this?

My interviews pinpointed seven best practices, which should be implemented to narrow the gap between top managers and salespeople, the leaders and their army, the decision makers and the executers, head office and the stores.

1. Visit your teams in the field

If you take over a brand's top management, there is no time to lose: you must visit your points of sale. One of your top priorities should be to connect with your sales force and be a role model. This will allow you to create personal bonds with all your teams right from the start, which is important in a transition period. Salespeople need to be reassured and are eager to meet their new guide, as s/he will help them reach the brand's essence.

Whenever you are in a country in which your brand is present, don't forget to meet with your sales team. If they learn that you were in the area, but did not even find a minute to pass by the store, this can lead to immeasurable demotivation.

> *As Vice President of Cartier, I opened many stores around the world. It was an important sign of respect to all my teams for me to visit them and their*

boutique as often as possible. In the evening, after store closure, I took them out for a drink in a bistro or hotel. This was always the best moment for them to share important messages and dare to speak up. Once back in the office, I then passed on the messages to the departments concerned with new input fresh from the field.

(Michel Guten, Sup de Luxe President,
Vice President Comité Champs-Élysées, former Vice President of Cartier)

You can win one year of motivation by visiting your sales teams. Some stores even kept the photos of my last visit in their boutique since they felt so honored that someone from the head office came to see them.

(Alexandre Fauvet,
former Executive Vice President at Lacoste)

And if top managers make the effort of knowing each employee by his or her name, this helps staff feel immeasurable respect for them and a real bond.

Jean Louis Dumas, former chairman of the Hermès Group, knew the first name of each employee, even the people working at the production sites. He was amazingly humble and had a great sense of humor. He greeted everyone, shook hands. He worked a lot, was a great speaker, close to his teams, a real president.

(Store manager at a high-end watchmaking brand)

2. Live their life

During periods of heavy commercial activity especially, show support for your teams. The best way to do this is to be present on the shopfloor. Even if you are the general manager and are not an excellent salesperson, the sales force would love to see you do their daily job! Not only would you experience the tough realities of sales, but you would also gain a lot of positive points from your teams.

Even though I am not a very good salesperson, I helped selling ties and scarves in stores during Christmastime. The salespeople had so much fun seeing me struggling with difficult customers or when preparing nice presents and gift boxes. This also helped me understand the difficulties of this profession, standing all day long, serving the customer in the most welcoming and convincing way. I did not do this to show off, but to really get a feel for sales and the teams.

(Christian Blanckaert, Professor in Luxury Management at ESCP Europe and former CEO of Hermès Sellier and Hermès International)

For marketing managers, selling should be on their monthly schedule. It's only by experiencing life on the floor that they can get a clearer idea of the customer and salespeople's needs, merchandising requirements and their competitors' marketing activities.

Besides gaining positive points from the teams and knowledge about the field, if managers demonstrate excellence in selling, they would be highly respected. In this way a person who has a thorough knowledge of what selling is all about can gain legitimacy as a top manager.

Even as President of Richemont, I went to sell in the field. It was very important to show salespeople that I was one of them, so that they understand why I had the right to shout at them sometimes. Salespeople can try to find hundreds of excuses for low performance. They can be extremely creative in this respect. They are clever, like cats. But you can also easily manipulate them. When you are used to working in the field, you immediately detect what is true or just a lie. People at Richemont told me that I was wasting my time by spending so much time on the sales force. Then I explained that they were wrong for two reasons: first of all because I come from the field, these are my roots and I therefore need to stay in touch with them. Secondly, I want to be respected by my salespeople in the same way that I respect them. I want to show them that I know their job at least as well as they do. This is essential. This is important.

(Alain Dominique Perrin, Non-Executive Director at Richemont Group, former President at Cartier International, President of EFMD (European Foundation for Management Development) and President of EDC (École des Dirigeants et Créateurs d'Entreprises))

However, selling, as a top manager, is not recommended in all cultures. In Asia, especially in China, Japan, Korea or Taiwan, this can be perceived as interfering with a salesperson's profession. It can be seen as not trusting the expertise of the sales force, which may even lead to a salesperson losing face. In these cultures, top management should accompany salespeople and encourage them, but not try to prove that they can do the salesperson's job.

3. Organize feedback meetings

It is essential to bring your sales teams together regularly in order to listen to their market reality. This can be done through conference calls with your shop managers or regional directors, depending on your company's organization. Even though conference calls are convenient, they don't replace physical meetings at the head office, at which the ups and downs of the brand and the emotions of its leaders can be felt. The frequency and time frame of these feedback sessions depend on the size of your team and the brand activity. For example, meetings need to be planned immediately after having launched a product, in order to readjust the launch strategy if necessary.

> *During launch periods I organized team meetings every week. All of my salespeople in wholesale came to Paris and we met late in the evening for between 45 and 60 minutes. We shared the positive and negative aspects of the launch in a very efficient and constructive discussion before I took them out for dinner. The organization was different for retail salespeople, who could not come to Paris during the week. Therefore, I received them in beautiful locations at weekends.*
>
> (Alain Dominique Perrin, Non-Executive Director at Richemont Group, former President at Cartier International, President of EFMD (European Foundation for Management Development) and President of EDC (École des Dirigeants et Créateurs d'Entreprises))

4. Develop brainstorming sessions

Before starting new operational measures for your brand, it is recommended managers collaborate closely with the people directly involved in the day-to-day business. When you allow them to share their best-practice experiences and when you listen to them, you can be sure that the new guidelines will be adopted.

> *We rounded up all our shop managers in order to elaborate Robert Clergerie's new selling ritual. First, we listened to everyone's selling experiences with the brand before we defined the main steps in the selling ritual for high-end shoes. In luxury, it is important to choose the right words at the right moment. We therefore identified the words and sentences that fitted best for our brand. It was very efficient to have participants work in two teams; with each team then being shown the other's ideas. Once all steps, words and sentences were defined, we started writing the sales ritual concept. Here again, it was important to write out the ritual in close collaboration with our sales managers in order to insure full clarity throughout the implementation period.*
>
> (Elodie Leprince-Ringuet, International Retail Director at Robert Clergerie, former Bonpoint European Retail Director)

5. Distribute feedback questionnaires

This method allows you to structure your feedback process by asking your sales team precise questions that are related to a topic relevant to them, for instance, the latest product launch. Clearly indicate what you want to know and the deadline by which they need to respond. This strategy reduces the possibility of useless complaints and inefficient critique, which is always a danger if managers open up the field too widely. There also are issues for which you may not favor the sales force's input, such as product development, which remains the brand creator's responsibility. Salespeople can suggest ways to sell a product but not necessarily how to create it. This is a line that needs to be drawn by management. Therefore, targeted questionnaires clearly indicate in which fields you appreciate input and where the limits are.

> *I created feedback questionnaires when I noticed that salespeople were complaining about product creations. I did not want to hear that the product was too big, too small or too green. I wanted to know how to sell it more efficiently. The product is the brand. When you buy a car, you don't change its engine. The questionnaire allowed me to ask precise questions to get the information I needed from my sales teams. Their*

answers were extremely helpful for further brand development with regard to products, strategies, processes.

(Alain Dominique Perrin, Non-Executive Director at Richemont Group, former President of Cartier International, President of EFMD (European Foundation for Management Development) and President of EDC (École des Dirigeants et Créateurs d'Entreprises))

6. Open door policy

An open door policy does not mean that you should allow your sales teams to step into your office whenever they want. It means that you are willing to listen and welcome constructive ideas from those in the field. Companies that do not encourage their sales teams to communicate from the bottom up don't generate as many innovative ideas as those who do. Salespeople should not be afraid of being punished for sharing ideas about the brand's future development.

> *I encourage my salespeople to share their ideas with me, since the truth comes from the field. This is reality. However, I am very respectful toward my retail managers. Whenever I get direct information from the field, I make sure I reintegrate the information within the regular communication channels. More specifically, I let my managers know who had the original idea and ask their opinion before implementing. It is essential to show interest in others and to value their ideas. For instance, when I present a new concept that was born in the field, I let everyone know who the originator was. Never give the impression that you are the one who came up with the idea alone, since this is rarely true. The best ideas are usually generated at the base and in the team.*
>
> (Natalie Bader, CEO of Prada France, former President at Fred International, former Marketing Director at Sephora)

An open door policy also means that urgent matters can be taken directly to the top without needing to pass through multiple layers first. This direct warning system can be very reassuring for salespeople. Whenever there is an important quality issue, salespeople feel justified in sending a direct e-mail to their CEO, copying in the store manager. It is fatal for the brand's health if quality issues are not solved immediately.

> *In the US, Starbucks had implemented a very strong open door policy for customers. The district manager in charge of around 1700 Starbucks in New York and its surrounding areas had left his business cards on counters inviting customers to call directly if they were dissatisfied. Why not implement a similar tool for salespeople? Wouldn't this be exceptional?*
> (Arnaud Vidal, former Vice President Watches and Jewelry at Ralph Lauren and former General Manager of Audemars Piguet)

7. One-on-one meetings

Not everything can be dealt with in group settings, since all salespeople have their own personalities, problems, concerns, wishes and aspirations. Therefore, managers should make themselves available for precious individual face time. If you can, establish regular time slots dedicated to your sales force, like a doctor in his practice; this is the ideal situation.

> *Whenever salespeople request a personal meeting in order to share preoccupations, it is important to react quickly. Making them wait too long stirs up anger, frustration and demotivation – feelings that must be avoided if a brand wants to be successful. I was extremely organized when it came to meetings with my team. My assistant planned three to four hours each day that were dedicated to individual meetings. Between two and four pm, I received non-managers and urgent cases and, between six and eight pm, I dealt with managers and the less urgent cases. Since I begin my day very early and finish late, I always had enough time to receive my sales force.*
> (Alain Dominique Perrin, Non-Executive Director at Richemont Group, former President of Cartier International, President of EFMD (European Foundation for Management Development) and President of EDC (École des Dirigeants et Créateurs d'Entreprises))

Beyond having individual "visiting" hours during the year, one-on-one meetings should also take place twice a year, for supervisory interviews. Dare to set up a 360-degree approach in which you listen to your sales teams and they listen to you. This is an effective way to set common goals, share ideas, exchange information and work well together in the future.

This is how one of Cartier's sales managers put it:

> *If our managers listen and don't shout at us when something is not 100 percent perfect, we feel respected and motivated, and can leave our personal problems at the door of our boutique more easily.*

Heart-winner 17: Reward your teams!

In heart-winner 3, I analyzed the compensation systems that allow managers to keep salespeople's fire burning. Since it is expected that work will be rewarded by compensation, extra monetary rewards are unlikely to generate long-lasting emotions and thus strong brand relationships. Instead, managers need to be careful about the way they set up compensation systems in order to prevent fires from dying out.

In this chapter, I want to focus on the compensation tools that truly affect feelings of recognition and emotional bonds with brands. My interviews with salespeople revealed that non-monetary, unexpected attentions had the highest effect upon salespeople's positive relationship with their brands. The gifts that generate the strongest emotions aren't always the most expensive ones. What matters is the personal touch.

Simple thank-you notes from the brand president for great sales achievements or special personal occasions are perceived as an incredible honor. If they are handwritten on nice paper with, in addition, a beautiful bouquet of flowers, the effect is even greater. Flowers are a particularly emotive gift due to their sensory nature. They are aesthetic and can be chosen and arranged to match the style of your brand.

> *While I was working for Chaumet and Cartier, the ladies were offered lovely flowers for their anniversaries; the men got wine of the highest quality. These kinds of attentions from our president showed me that*

ILL 14 / Because you are worth it!

(Source: Albert Dessinateur for Michaela Merk)

these brands knew how to say 'thank you.' This kind of recognition is key to binding your salespeople to your brand. It is not very complicated, but it needs to be done and it makes a difference.

(Store manager at a high-end watchmaking brand)

A store manager at Fendi still talks about the gift she received for great achievements with nostalgia:

Stuffed toys were given to the whole team when we obtained the best progression rate last year. We felt so proud that we decided to create a Facebook fan page for our mascots, which are still displayed in our store.

A store manager at Sonia Rykiel told me about her ritual of opening a bottle of champagne at the end of a successful day, which resembles

Sonia Rykiel's festive way of saying thank you to her team at the end of the year with unforgettable celebrations.

Quite apart from gifts, private sales are also a highly appreciated sign of recognition. While salespeople usually cannot afford to buy the brand's products for use in their private lives, price reductions for employees allow them to buy other brand products at cheaper prices.

But the most appreciated gifts seem to be those which are totally unexpected.

> *My brand had set up surprise rewards for exceptional months in terms of sales results. A present was sent by top management to each salesperson from the successful store, such as a gift vouchers worth €300, for example. It's like in your own personal relationships: gifts for your birthday are expected. However, thoughtful and unexpected surprises give you even more joy than the expected ones.*
>
> (Store manager at a high-end jewelry brand)

Another efficient way of rewarding your teams is to give them the feeling of "being chosen." This can be done by selecting one store as a best-practice reference for all other stores within the brand. These kinds of selections can be orchestrated by organizing competitions to design, for instance, the most creative shop window in order to obtain the highest number of new customers. Other ideas could include developing the best training tools for newcomers or demonstrating the best service level. Being chosen also makes it clear that the top management pays special attention to exceptional talent or skills within the profession. A former Repetto sales representative told me:

> *I felt extremely honored when our president came to visit our store with a very good American client. Among the 15 salespeople who were serving in our store, he chose me to serve this customer and her daughter. When he said "I want Raphael to take care of this customer", you cannot imagine how honored I felt at that moment.*

And finally, a brand can invite both customers and salespeople to many types of events. For customers, these events are flattering since the brand thanks them for their loyalty. For salespeople these events are memorable moments when exceptional performance is recognized.

> *As former Vice President of Ralph Lauren Watches, I often invited our salespeople to have dinner with me in outstanding restaurants. It was fundamental to spend quality time with them, since many human resources consultancy firms were greatly interested in them. Besides, when I was invited to VIP events, I sometimes allowed my salespeople to attend those events with their best clients. Not only did they feel honored to be invited by the president, but this was also an efficient method by which to strengthen the sales force–customer bond.*
>
> (Arnaud Vidal, former Vice President Watches and Jewelry at Ralph Lauren and former General Manager of Audemars Piguet)

Filled with nostalgia, a former Prada store manager expressed her enthusiasm for Prada's store-opening celebrations:

> *When we opened the store in the prestigious Rue du Faubourg Saint-Honoré in Paris, Mrs. Prada organized a dinner party at the Iéna Palace. At first, a small circle of invited guests dined with Mrs. Prada. Later in the evening, more guests as well as salespeople were invited for dancing. Those who came early enough even had a chance to see Mrs. Prada dining. It was an extreme honor to be so close to the person who creates all those amazing styles. The place was simply magnificent.*

Heart-winner 18: Make your people grow!

Many brands lose their sales force because they are unable to provide an honest perspective on the possibilities for career development. It is a human need to define one's path, to know where to go, to climb the career ladder, to fulfill dreams and goals. When aspiring to be successful, there also is a strong desire to grow intellectually, to learn and to progress.

It is a real challenge for brands and companies to satisfy these fundamental human needs. It is clearly impossible to promote all those who wish to be promoted from a salesperson to a senior sales advisor, to department manager, to store manager and so on. It is therefore important to

ILL 15 / Make your people grow!

(Source: Albert Dessinateur for Michaela Merk)

find alternative ways to satisfy your sales force in order to maintain their motivation and aspiration to serve your brand over the long run. My interviews with salespeople clearly showed that brand relationships were often wrecked when hopes and promises remained unfulfilled.

I have identified four strategies that allow salespeople to grow without having to promise all of them that they will reach management positions in the future. This would be totally unrealistic due to sheer numbers, plus the fact that it is only certain people who have the ability to become top managers. The following people-development strategy points to four paths you can recommend to your salespeople. Each path leads to a different kind of professional profile and always needs to be carefully evaluated with respect to each individual. So, before you send a salesperson on his/her journey, some observation time is required in order to take the right decision and direct them to the right path. These kinds of decisions are usually taken in collaboration with human resources, retail and general management. They are crucial for your company's success since they can considerably impact on your team and their relationship with the company. Your brand's reputation, and its status as a potential employer, are also in play.

The first path is called INCOMPATIBILITY and leads to the DROPOUT of the salesperson

This is an unfortunate but important path to take if there is an incompatibility between a salesperson and your brand. Incompatibility can be related to a mismatch in terms of values, performance, character, expectations or skills. Not everyone has the qualities needed to become a salesperson. Learning to become a good salesperson is not easy since selling is very personal. Many excellent salespeople told me that selling needed to be in your DNA for you to become a successful salesperson. Incompatible matches need to be identified and the extent of the incompatibility assessed. If there is a wide gap between the targeted and actual result, managers must have the courage to be honest with their teams. Instead of letting salespeople expect something that will never happen, it is advisable to tell them the truth. But there are various ways to tell the truth. If you lay someone off without any explanation or by making him/her feel at fault, you violently sever links with the employee, and this may endanger your brand. If you are unable to respond to a salesperson's expectations, it is important to act quickly. An unsatisfied salesperson on the floor can be like an unexploded bomb if you don't detect the problem in time. There are multiple dangers: a salesperson who cuts ties with the brand can spread a negative attitude among clients and colleagues. The danger of contamination is huge, like a bacteria that spreads at high speed in warm temperatures. Since salespeople spend a lot of time together, negative influencers can be highly devastating for the group. Many brands wait too long, either because they don't see the potential bomb or because they are not courageous enough to eliminate it.

> My recommendation is to be extremely honest and transparent to salespeople who seem to have unrealistic aspirations. Let them know that they are good, but also say clearly that you won't be thinking of them if a specific position opened up. In my past career, I experienced exactly such an unfortunate case. Because of frequent rotations, a salesperson

had replaced store managers several times, hoping to be nominated store manager herself one day. She had been waiting to obtain this position for a long time. Unfortunately, she wasn't the right fit but no one had the courage to tell her the truth: you won't get this position now or five years from now. So when I told her, it was too late. She had been waiting for over six years and her frustration was immense. She felt fooled by the company and therefore started talking negatively about the brand to clients and colleagues. It even became a legal case. The result was a disaster for everyone.

(Arnaud Vidal, former Vice President Watches and Jewelry at Ralph Lauren and former General Manager of Audemars Piguet)

The second path is TALENT DEVELOPMENT and leads to the world of STARS

In sales, we call them star salespeople: they are the ones who have it in their blood. The challenge then becomes to help them progress, help them improve their selling skills, achieve higher sellout figures, attract the super-rich clients and expand their customer portfolio in terms of quality and quantity. In short: you need to strengthen overachievers. Such employees need to be pampered, since they generate business. You definitely don't want to lose them. So what can be done in order to strengthen their ties with your brand and to give them the feeling of being respected by management?

In their case, the best recipe is training, training, training.

Both perceived and actual knowledge gaps should be identified before determining the kind of training that should be provided. I distinguish perceived knowledge from actual knowledge, since salespeople aren't always aware of their true weaknesses. Generally, salespeople tend to have strong personalities and a positive opinion of themselves. It is therefore the manager's role to put them in front of a mirror, showing them what reality looks like. Understanding reality is the basis of progress.

Providing individual coaching by professional external coaches is an efficient tool for future star salespeople. The term "coach" derives from sports. The coach is a person who observes you, corrects you, and accompanies you along the way to success. He prepares your career path, is a mentor,

ILL 16 The Star-salesperson

(Source: Albert Dessinateur for Michaela Merk)

a guide, a person of trust, and a role model, a true expert. When I was training for the German Gymnastics Championships, I had several coaches who had to catch hold of me many times before I was able to perform the exercises alone. Their assistance was essential to keep me on track without losing precious time.

In sales, it is the coach's role to identify the areas in which a salesperson needs to improve. This can result in product, brand, sales technique or

ILL 17 / Coaching session

(Source: Albert Dessinateur for Michaela Merk)

service training, depending on the individual situation. If you provide tailor-made training, it is important to assess improvements on a regular basis. Training alone won't suffice. Again, in sports you always need to compare your past and present results. When you train for the 100m sprint, after having received new input from your coach it is helpful to compare your previous time with your latest one. This practice is stimulating and motivating and is used as an indicator to improve your performance.

We organized monthly coaching sessions in the stores, which go hand in hand with the individual interviews salespeople have with their managers. These are interviews based upon factual KPIs. These indicators allow us to clearly identify strengths and weaknesses, points of excellence and potential areas for improvement. For instance, we could tell a salesperson that his overall results during the previous month were great, but that we noticed that he only tended to sell handbags instead of venturing into other product categories. The salesperson then sees clearly that he needs to improve when selling other product categories, such as shoes. Excellent salespeople manage to fascinate clients who end up willing to buy products in multiple categories. It is the salesperson's role to show them possible product combinations, make them feel that one product is much nicer when accompanied by another one. In conjunction with the coaches, our managers help salespeople to get to know themselves better and improve in all fields.

(Natalie Bader, CEO of Prada France,
former President at Fred International and
former Marketing Director at Sephora)

Interviews of salespeople take place once or twice a year in most companies. These are important in order to balance targets and actual achievements. Yet salespeople live in the present. They are operational doers rather than strategic thinkers. Their reality is now. This is why correcting them on the spot is essential in order to make them see their mistakes and correct them immediately.

Once a salesperson has successfully been through the training sessions on offer, don't forget to present a diploma. This is a symbolic but important tool of recognition. Symbols and signs are tangible and allow us to show that "I made it!" This piece of paper does not cost a lot and makes a big difference when it comes to building relationships between brands and their salespeople. Over 1000 certificates were handed over during the Olympic Games in London in order to honor sportsmen and women for excellent performances. Why not do so after successful training sessions, in which salespeople give their best to improve, excel, impress?

Besides arranging coaching sessions and issuing diplomas, you can also organize high-level brainstorming sessions with your star salespeople. Gather them together from time to time and let them discuss a problem, a strategic issue related to their field where improvements are required. Exchanges with other top sellers can be extremely beneficial since sharing your vision with others helps you to form new constructive ideas for your brand. Your salespeople will be more aware of the reasons for their success and the progress they still have to make. They will also learn from others, who are as brilliant as they are. Stars learn from stars. Whenever you bring the best together, winning strategies tend to be the result.

The third possible path is called DISCOVERY and helps to develop ALL-ROUNDERS

All-rounders also have a very important role to play within a company. They can take on various roles whenever needed. In our fast-changing retail environment especially, brands are facing new challenges. It is important to react quickly. This requires flexible structures where your brand can change, expand and improve constantly. In order to implement change, you need people who follow a lead without complaining. While super salespeople are more linear and aim to develop in one direction – having the highest turnover possible – all-rounders fulfill another, as important, role for healthy and consistent brand evolution. By nature, these people are keen to discover and learn new things. They are curious and don't mind leaving their dedicated task in order to take up new responsibilities. They are driven by a permanent desire to expand their intellectual horizon. This requires a certain flexibility. If you were to drop them in unknown waters, they would not drown but rather feel intense pleasure about experiencing a new adventure.

> In order to keep some of our salespeople loyal to our brand, we need to find new missions for them. These can be tasks such as training the sales team from a recently opened store or helping management in the

ILL 18 / The Allrounder-salesperson

(Source: Albert Dessinateur for Michaela Merk)

opening process of a new international store. The person could dedicate himself to a new store before coming back to his original point of sale. It must be clear from the beginning that there is a way back once the mission is completed.

> (Natalie Bader, CEO of Prada France,
> former President at Fred International and
> former Marketing Director at Sephora)

The all-rounder is similar to a consultant who steps in when needed, accomplishes the mission and then withdraws again from the operation. Their job and life can be very colorful since tasks can vary considerably. Usually, they are brilliant team players since they are usually very popular among their colleagues and easily fit into a new environment without long adaptation periods. Like a chameleon, they take up the colors of their surroundings. In cases of friction, they are the ones who manage to stop the fight, conciliate and establish peace again. Brands need such people in their teams in order to keep them balanced and stabilized.

The fourth path is called RESPONSIBILITY and directs a salesperson to a higher-ranking MANAGEMENT position

These people are the exception rather than the norm. It is quite rare for a salesperson to show such exceptional top management qualities that s/he is promoted to higher-ranking responsibilities. These rare people are the ones who are great at rallying team members, thinking ahead, putting present ideas into clearly structured concepts, revealing a visionary spirit and highlighting the big picture in any given situation.

All these skills are not necessarily required to be a good salesperson. However, they are essential for being a successful brand leader guiding large teams. If these talents emerge, they should not be left on the shopfloor since such people have a different role to play for the company. Yet whatever salespeople learn on the field is extremely helpful in their future career path in order to take the correct, best-adapted decisions for the brand. For that reason it is advisable for every future manager to experience work on the shopfloor. This is where you learn about the reality of the brand, your customers and your competitors' way of presenting their products in the points of sale.

> *There are two groups among the world's big leaders: the former salespeople and the technocrats. The second group is quite large. The first group, however, is mostly made of leaders who manage to achieve sky-rocketing success for their companies, since they know the reality and tactics of sales. Yet being a good salesperson requires different skills to being a good leader. Salespeople who are too ambitious and believe they can become the brand's CEO simply because they generate huge sales are even dangerous. To manage people, you need tremendous experience in leadership, and you need to be visionary, willing to take over responsibilities. Success is shared, failure is not.*
>
> (Alain Dominique Perrin, Non-Executive Director at Richemont Group,
> former President of Cartier International,
> President of EFMD (European Foundation for Management Development)
> and President of EDC (École des Dirigeants et Créateurs d'Entreprises))

Top management, working together with the retail and human resources departments, must closely observe members in your team in order to define their future path. The four possible routes are displayed below in the shape of crossroads that illustrate each salesperson's career path and evolution (Figure 18). The best direction doesn't simply depend upon each salesperson's individual ambitions but on each person's character, since personality predefines one's path. Each brand and company must nurture their staff so that each person can walk along the path that truly suits them best. Salespeople will then feel fulfilled, happy, enjoy their daily tasks and remain loyal to their employer.

Table 3 assembles character traits that may help human resources and retail managers distinguish between potential STARS and ALL-ROUNDERS. Certainly, this table is not meant to be black or white. All-rounders may

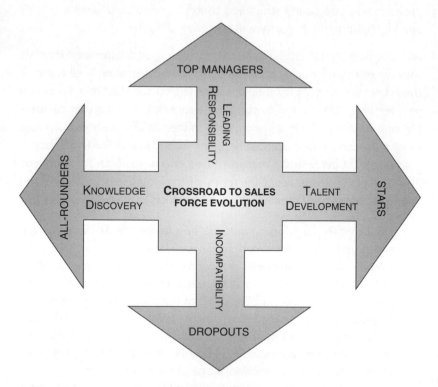

FIG 18   The crossroads to sales force evolution

Table 3   Salesperson characteristics of all-rounders and stars

All-Rounders	Stars
Curious	Ambitious
Flexible	Competitive
Open-minded	Goal-driven
Multi-tasking	Straightforward
Cultivated	Mysterious
Conciliating	Tactical
Harmonious	Perfectionist
Balanced	Individual
Team-building	Passionate
Adventurous	Expert

share some characteristics of Stars and vice versa. However, it should help illustrate where the big differences can be found.

This list is not exhaustive and could be extended. It principally shows how different these two sales personalities are. Crucially, these two types perceive recognition differently. In order to adapt the brand's reward system accordingly, it is important to discover which employees belong to which category.

One character trait, however, is common to both populations: empathy! Being able to empathize is essential for understanding customers, reading their desires, detecting their needs and translating all of this information into a successful sales ritual that culminates into a transaction.

Fundamental errors can be made when companies start treating everyone in the same way. As luxury brands are a people business, characters make the game; they are like colorful spices that make dishes tasty and interesting. Top management must therefore find tailor-made growth strategies for people. Otherwise, the brand will become a boring soup which looks and tastes like many others. Each company needs to stand out from the crowd, to cultivate unique brand concepts and employee development strategies. To do so, managers need to be visionary and courageous. They must be aware that their brand can only grow if they allow its people to grow. And they should also realize that they can grow themselves when their people grow around them.

In dealing with such notions of people development, the manager becomes an important role model. By looking at a brand's performance, you can tell if the brand has a good relationship with its sales force. Leaders who make their people grow bring their teams to higher levels of performance. They are charismatic and hold the brand's flag with a clear conviction of its superiority and with a desire to win against competitors – but always within a team. They are aware that no champions succeed without an excellent coach.

This is what good management is all about: make your teams grow and you will grow with them. I understand that I am nothing without the others around me. It is therefore very important to respect them, to listen to them and to demonstrate managerial courage. I have worked with many managers in my past but I have not met many courageous ones. I am fully convinced that managers need to be extremely brave in order to say what they truly think to others. It is important to be honest, transparent, factual and clear. The relationships salespeople have with their brands are more likely to break down if you wait too long to tell them the truth. It will come out one day anyway. A lot also depends upon the way you convey a message. You can criticize someone without hurting him/her but, instead, by reinforcing their own awareness of reality. Instead of trying to work on someone's weaknesses, which you could probably never transform into strengths, detect their strengths and make those stronger. This is the best way to make your teams progress. In the worst cases, you may need to part ways with some staff members. But you can at least allow your people to understand your decision. When you show managerial courage, your teams will respect you. They know that you are on the front line and always the first to assume failures and celebrate victories. I was always lucky that my teams were willing to follow me all along my career path.

(Natalie Bader, CEO of Prada France,
former President at Fred International
and former Marketing Director at Sephora)

This is often true but unfortunate: bad managers have bad salespeople. This can be seen at all company levels. Putting a good manager in place can allow the brand to grow by more than 30 percent. I experienced this throughout my career: when you change a badly performing team, your sales improve considerably. This problem might be related to a single person who needs to be identified. Yet a salesperson who performs badly for one brand won't necessarily perform poorly for another brand. I have seen this happen many times, when there is an incompatibility between cultures and values.

(Christian Blanckaert, Professor in Luxury Management at ESCP Europe and former CEO of Hermès Sellier and Hermès International)

chapter 3

Ways of Winning Over the Sales Force in the Digital World

The omnipresence of digital tools in our lives is fundamentally changing the retail environment, its rules and actors. It is one of the megatrends of the 21st century, heavily influencing and modifying the given structures of shopping and consumption. Digitalization is invading all areas of our lives at such speed that many companies have trouble keeping up.

Customers consuming exclusively in physical stores belong to the past. Shopping and navigating across multiple online and offline channels has become the norm, and customers have been faster at adapting to the new environment of technology than most luxury brands. Many brands remained skeptical for a long time, believing that the traditional luxury world and the digital world were incompatible. Today, however, they realize that they need to catch up if they do not want to lose sight of reality. Internet Pure Players have taken the opportunity of filling the gap and giving the luxury customer what luxury brands themselves could not offer: a unique digital shopping experience across multiple channels with fully integrated customer data.

Luxury brands are now starting to jump onto the digital train that is already moving at high speed throughout the world. In some countries, such as China and the USA, it is at its peak speed.

While luxury brands have understood that digitalization is no longer an option but a must, they are now confronted with three major challenges (Figure 19):

1. Interconnection of retail channels

One challenge is, of course, to develop all new sales channels that are requested by the modern customer: mobile and desktop shopping platforms which provide technological efficiency, safety and also a unique brand-related shopping experience. At the same time, physical stores are still an essential retail channel, since customers constantly cross borders between the online and offline world. Companies need, therefore, to find ways of intelligently integrating and interconnecting all retail realities within one common ecosystem.

2. Integration and management of customer data

Another challenge is to integrate the customer into the brand's communication flow and structure and analyze the data in the best-targeted way in order to favor a one-on-one marketing approach. As communication switches from being a one-way brand–customer interaction into a two-way brand–customer–brand flow, brands are beginning to get to know their customers again. But such a massive concentration of data needs to be prepared and used in the most appropriate way according to the brand's positioning. This fundamental change also alters the way companies practice marketing, since larger and larger budgets are being allocated to digital channels. These channels have their own laws, which are not terribly well known and are rapidly changing environments.

3. Association of the sales force

Changing customer habits and the emergence of new retail channels have had a considerable impact on the sales force. Salespeople find themselves confronted with customers who are perfectly informed about the brand since they have found accurate data online. It has become common to go online to get a perfect overview of the market before shopping offline. Sometimes salespeople even find themselves less informed than their customers.

Furthermore, compensation strategies are not currently well adapted to the new retail reality. Consequently, salespeople have trouble integrating the

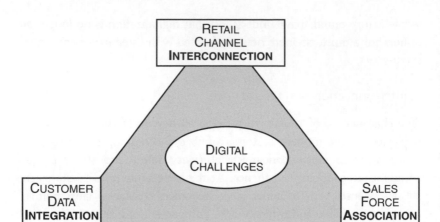

FIG 19 The digital impact on retail channels, customers and sales force

digital shopping environment with their own retail scope. Many find that helping their brand develop digital channels isn't in their interest, since this might have a negative effect on their own brick-and-mortar sales results. From a management point of view, both worlds are still treated separately, which does not help when attempting to merge online and offline channels. It is therefore important for companies to fully associate their sales force with their digital projects instead of treating them as the "offline sales team."

While brands are confronted with these major challenges, which stem from the increasing omnipresence of digital reality, the question is: How can digital tools help to strengthen salespeople's relationships with their brands?

To answer this question, I want to illustrate my vision with the example of the five rings of sales force–brand relationships, which are essential means by which to tie salespeople to your brand.

3.1   Love-booster: Digital media to pass on the flame

In order to enflame salespeople's love for their brand, communication must be fluid within the entire organization. Internal communication structures must be set up and clearly defined in order for employees to be informed, to learn, to exchange and to share. Let them know immediately anything that concerns your brand, its values, strategies, ongoing changes, events, new products, new people, as long as this information is not fundamentally confidential. The communication style that is most valued corresponds to four criteria:

1. honesty
2. transparency
3. accuracy
4. fluidity.

The time factor is essential in order to make sure that your employees, including your sales force, are always the first to be informed, well before anyone else, such as customers or the press. Unfortunately, salespeople are too often unable to give precise information on their brand's online shop. The brand managers therefore need to stimulate salespeople's awareness of the fact that this sales channel is also part of their concern. This requires the setup of fast, efficient and interactive communication devices. Digital tools are invaluable in helping companies spread messages faster than ever before and ensuring that departments on different hierarchy levels are interconnected. Just as communication between brands and their customers becomes increasingly interactive, we can observe the same trend within companies. One-sided, top-down communication patterns belong to the past – interactivity is the present and future (Figure 20).

> *When I was a retail manager for Yves Saint Laurent, I always dreamt of using the iPad to connect the retail space of all our boutiques to the head office. I imagined a platform where we could upload merchandising visuals, training tools, brand visuals, logos, presentations and so on. It would have been great to bring everyone closer together, accelerate exchanges between all departments: managers, buyers, merchandising, communication and sales. This would have been extremely convenient, especially for stores that are far away from the head office, in Cannes, Monaco or anywhere else in the world. Sharing information via the iPad would have allowed us to gain time and to increase real face time.*
> (Jean-Charles Champey, former Store Manager at Yves Saint Laurent)

Social media such as Facebook and Twitter are not only useful to make customers like your brand and share exciting brand content. They can also be fabulous tools with which to foster internal communication.

> *Our new communication director put in place daily teasers the week before our big fashion show. The teasers, like a countdown, were sent*

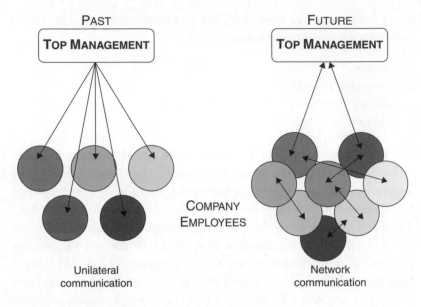

FIG 20 / **Changing company communication patterns**

to the entire company, including the sales force. They contained little videos, barely longer than two minutes, to attract our attention to the brand-related content: words, sentences, interviews in which Sonia Rykiel explained her vision, style, her way to design. These were remixed extracts of existing documentaries. Sometimes, he also sent some of Sonia's drawings before she finalized her creations. This was an amazing means by which to bring us closer to the brand's origin in a visual, modern and interesting way.

(Shayda de Bary, Store Manager at Sonia Rykiel)

Salespeople constantly need to share. Because of the nature of their profession and the type of personality it attracts, salespeople should be good listeners and communicators. By allowing them to interconnect through an internal digital platform, they would have the opportunity to exchange information on customer experiences, best practices, ideas, failures and learnings. Such a social platform would allow them to realize the fact that they all have similar experiences and somehow belong to a big family. By forming a genuine digital community, an internal social media platform could help strengthen your salespeople's relationships among each other and with your brand.

One of the first brands to put in place a digital platform for salespeople was Burberry. Angela Ahrendts, former CEO of Burberry, talked about this positive achievement in the mini movie "Burberry's Social Story," saying:

> *The next generation is going to grow up in a digital world. And they speak social. Whenever you are talking to customers or employees, you have to do it on a social platform because that's the language they speak. We were one of the first to customize the chatter platform – we call it Burberry chat. Christopher and I chat with the entire organization once or twice a week. It also gives each associate a platform to talk to us. Most importantly, it has been the greatest unifier of our culture in comparison to any other platform we have ever put in place.*
> (http://www.youtube.com/watch?v=DzBIYwZsut0)

Instead of using traditional e-mail, instant messaging systems are becoming a more and more common way for employees to relate to each other. They allow quick question and answer exchanges without taking the time to formulate long, polite sentences. While form used to be extremely important in former company communications, the instant content, quick messages and fast answers are much more valued today. In internal communication, love for the brand will not be kindled through romantic words but rather thanks to the message's accuracy.

3.2 Identification-booster: Explaining omnichannel strategies

Over the course of my interviews, I came across two kinds of salespeople: the people in favor of digital improvements and those against.

The people against digitalization are mostly experienced and senior salespeople who have grown up in the company and are perfectly familiar with the traditional brick-and-mortar retail model. The digital world is quite distant from them. They expressed a certain degree of disappointment when their management decided to open a digital store and advocate e-commerce as the core focus of tomorrow. To these salespeople, the digital world is the enemy of the physical world. They regard e-shops as competitors of traditional retail and are therefore fully against it.

> *I feel that e-commerce goes against our profession, since the luxury business is based on relationships, service and human contact. It is always frustrating for a salesperson who spends a lot of time advising the customer and providing high-quality service, to finally find s/he has bought a product online based on the advice s/he received at the store.*
>
> (Store manager at a luxury jewelry brand)

The people that are pro-digitalization are mostly younger salespeople who already are digitally connected in their personal lives. They consider e-commerce to be complementary to their own stores and are fully aware of the advantages of digital commerce. For them, online shops have the capacity to attract a new customer base that may have remained untouched because of geographic or psychological reasons.

> *I believe that e-commerce represents a complementary sales channel to our stores. Many customers check out the new and existing collections online before they come to us. They have done half of the work we used to do, since they are perfectly informed. In our stores, they want to get a confirmation that they are making the best choice in terms of materials or colors, since images online are not always identical to reality. Before buying, customers love to touch their product. They come to confirm their choice rather than to get more information. This shift in customer habits is a big change compared to the past. We also have customers who come to our stores but are still hesitant to buy, mostly for money reasons. They think they might have a higher budget in the coming month in order to purchase the bag they like. So instead of having to go back to the store, they have the second option of buying online, which is very convenient. And, finally, we have customers who simply don't dare step into our stores and prefer buying online in order not to be seen.*
>
> (Longchamp store manager)

> *I don't believe that e-commerce is a threat, since, at least for jewelry, customers need to come to our stores to try the products on before they purchase.*

Then they have two options: to buy online or offline. But they have at least come to us once, to the base, to find the best fit.

(Fred sales associate)

Even though more and more salespeople have a favorable attitude toward their brand's digital stores, they are still far from identifying with them. Their brand reality is the physical stores where they welcome, advise and serve their customers. The e-shop is, for most of them, far away; somewhere at the brand's head office (Figure 21). Yet in order to successfully implement multi- or omnichannel strategies, salespeople must bring both spheres together. They must understand that their entire sales area can be considerably expanded if online and offline environments are merged. It is not only technology that brings databases together and delivers products to all sales channels. Omnichannel success also happens when salespeople are involved. If they begin to understand that their sales environment goes beyond their physical store, the brand will make a huge leap toward the retail reality of tomorrow.

FIG 21 The Sales force Identification Sphere (SIS)

What should brands do in order to expand salespeople's identification sphere from the physical to the digital shop? This question is essential since we know from the previous chapter that salespeople's hearts can be won if they identify with their point of sale. It's only if salespeople identify with the brand's online shops that these digital stores can help strengthen the relationship between salespeople and their brand (Figure 22).

The first step toward salespeople's e-identification is to explain the real online retail benefits through intense digital training. Even if salespeople already use digital tools, they may not have a clear picture of the true advantages, opportunities, challenges and strategies that will help the brand to grow. Every brand today should offer its salespeople general digital training

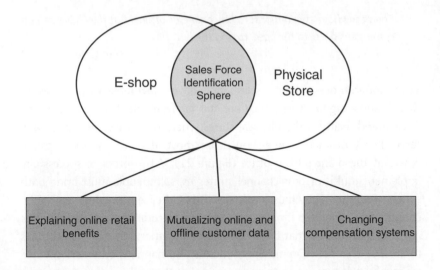

FIG 22 / **Factors influencing the Sales force Identification Sphere (SIS)**

including a particular focus on their brand's digital strategies. Experts need to explain to salespeople how omnichannel operations work and why they are in the brand's best interest. Provide relevant best-practice examples drawn from your competitors and other industries. Share facts and figures from existing digital studies. Lack of identification or even fear often derives from a lack of knowledge. It is therefore essential to close the knowledge gap before starting to implement digital channels and tools across the board. All salespeople should know their brand's online shop by heart.

The second step is to help salespeople understand that the brand's business can only grow if customer databases are shared. Until now, most salespeople have carefully protected their customer base and see it as their own asset. In the future, databases will need to be shared if brands want to access the customer's world, which is both online and offline. It's only when salespeople start thinking about the global benefits and not simply their local private business that they will begin to identify with the digital world.

The third step to sales force identification with e-commerce requires a radical change in compensation systems. As long as salespeople don't feel there is any benefit in advising customers to shop online or in sharing their offline customer database, there will probably be no progress in this identification process. Thus far, few companies have put in place compensation systems that consider the digital aspect of the brand. One reason for this is that brands must fully merge their online and offline customer data in order to conduct online and offline observations of their customers. In order to attribute online sales to a physical store, it is important to know to which store the customer belongs.

Pierre Laromiguière, President of Baobaz, a web-marketing agency, analyses the situation as follows:

> There is a real conflict between online and offline shops with regard to the management of the customer database. Many salespeople in the luxury industry are not willing to share their precious customer data with other salespeople as they consider their customers to 'belong' to them. They defend their territory as much as they can and only enter superficial data into the common database. Having a common, highly profiled customer database, however, is necessary for efficient multichannel operations. Tailor-made marketing activities could be put in place to incite customers to navigate smoothly between the online and offline universes of the brand. Thanks to digital cookies, it would then be easy to know when a person has been exposed to a Facebook, mailing or any other online campaign.
>
> Besides combining customer databases, a brand needs to review its compensation systems, which clearly depend on the possibility of allocating online sales to a specific physical store. In order to do so, brands would have to define an online market radius that leads to a physical store. This could be done by verifying the delivery address, which is provided during the checkout process for online sales. All purchases made by customers within a specific market radius would then be allocated to the respective stores. Consequently, the additional online sales would help the store increase its overall sales figures. The monthly commission for the entire team could then be based upon the sales achieved online and offline.

In the luxury sector, it makes a lot of sense for online sales to be allocated to an offline store, since customers tend to inform themselves online before buying offline. Many e-commerce sites therefore have a rather low transformation rate online but contribute to strong additional sales offline.

With online and offline shopping becoming increasingly interlinked, it is important to look at the pattern as a whole. In luxury, customers still prefer to check their preselection in the physical store and interact with a competent sales advisor. Consequently, expectations are high when customers do make the effort to go to the store, after having obtained all the information they need about the product they have chosen.

The multichannel market radius strategy (Figure 23) illustrates the fact that salespeople should apply new perspectives when it comes to sharing customer data and allocating cross-channel sales. Due to the new retail reality, brand management is confronted with the challenge of explaining the importance of changing mindsets to its sales force with regard to compensation and performance systems. The biggest challenge occurs when explaining this to the Star-salespeople with their giant, high-profile customer database, of which they are fiercely protective.

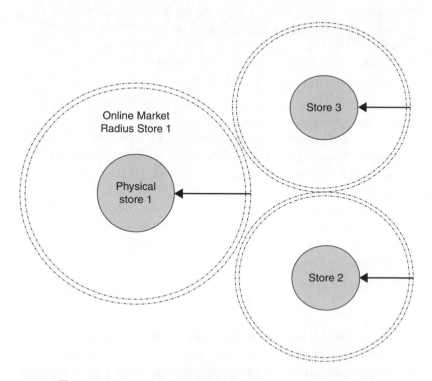

FIG 23 / **The multichannel market radius strategy**

I believe it is important to set up a multichannel sales approach, encouraging customers to check out the e-commerce site at the end of an in-store purchase: 'Madame, pretty soon the new collection will arrive. It is not in our store yet, but you can already view it online. I will send you the link of our e-commerce site and I remain available for any additional information. I will register you online so you can create your own personal space on our site. This will allow us to interact in case of questions, send images and simply be connected.' Not many brands have put in place a true omnichannel strategy. Besides the technical challenge, this new retail approach is complicated to set up due to questions related to sales commissions. Many salespeople today still see e-commerce as a real threat and not as a business opportunity. And since online shops can easily become as big as a flagship store, they are seen as fierce competitors. Whenever an offline customer shops online, it is considered as 'losing sales to the e-shop.'

(Jean-Charles Champey, former Store Manager at Yves Saint Laurent)

In order to encourage salespeople to orient their customers proactively towards the brand's e-commerce site or to order a product online for a customer, it is also advisable to link such actions to individual sales bonuses. This, however, is only possible if you can identify each salesperson online. It is therefore necessary to give a personal login and password to each sales associate as soon as s/he enters your brand's digital sales environment. Doing so will enable you to track salespeople who sell online or who add a customer to your brand's digital database. These actions are now part of modern selling rituals and need to be rewarded. If you don't do this, your sales force won't identify with your digital space and will always strictly separate the online and offline worlds.

3.3   Trust-booster: E-learning for faster knowledge

Training enhances salespeople's trust in their brand. This is what the previous chapter clearly demonstrated under heart-winner 8. Salespeople who have been perfectly trained by their brand in terms of sales arguments, products, the brand philosophy, sales objections and the sales ritual feel they can trust their brand. This creates a stronger relationship and leads to the development of a certain salesperson–brand loyalty.

The difficulty with the omnipresence of digital tools is that customers have multiple sources of information at their disposal. Before purchasing a luxury brand, they want to check out the collection, new arrivals, get detailed information on the new benefits and styles, and also compare prices. It has become natural to go online before buying offline. At the same time, customers trust brand-marketing statements less. They therefore need to know as much as possible before spending money. They simply don't want to be fooled.

Consequently, salespeople are confronted with customers who are already brand experts. Customers are extremely knowledgeable – at least on the product they intend to buy. This can be quite unpleasant for salespeople since multichannel luxury shoppers tend to test the sales force. Who is the bigger expert? What do I know that you don't know yet? In the worst case scenario, the customer doesn't even want any further advice since they already think they know everything. They have simply come to the store to see and handle the product in reality. This is unfortunately becoming more and more frequent, leaving salespeople somehow lost in translation. They begin to feel useless and incompetent, and lose faith in the brand that is supposed to provide them with relevant training.

> *The customer nowadays is ultra-informed thanks to the Internet. If he wants to access any kind of information, he navigates online. He tends to ask a lot more questions than several years ago. If the salesperson is not able to answer sophisticated customer questions, this reduces both the brand's and the salesperson's credibility.*
> (Alexandre Fauvet, former Executive Vice President at Lacoste)

In order to avoid such embarrassing situations, brands must intensify and anticipate their training on brand- and product-related issues. They must make sure that salespeople are the first to be informed, before the press or customers. While the geographic disparity of salespeople was a reason that once prevented them from all being updated at once, this is no longer an issue. E-learning tools allow all salespeople around the globe to find out about new products at the same time.

> *Before recent technology advanced in mobility and Cloud Commerce, sales associates used huge product books to learn about the features and benefits of the brand's merchandise. The books were labor-intensive to create and costly to distribute, and they often arrived in the store after the actual products. On top of that, the books were not convenient to use. As a result, product knowledge became lore, a word-of-mouth exercise with tenured associates teaching the new ones. Invariably, the lore changed a little with each telling, which led to a divergence from the original product script. Thanks to real-time product information available in the Cloud, e-learning applications on iPads can deliver all the necessary product-selling information on a single device in a fraction of the time. Any associates can use the information when they arc in a selling situation with a customer or when they need to familiarize themselves with new product assortments. Product-training departments can keep information accurate and timely, which is very important since product assortments change frequently. Dynamic brands are always on the move.*
> (Lawrence Grodzicki, Director Product Management Demandware, former E-commerce Project Manager and Retail Systems Expert at Timberland)

Yet, in order to make product training through e-learning efficient, it must be carefully organized and structured. It is the store manager's role to develop e-learning schedules which ensure that everyone is taking the necessary time to undergo the training.

> *In the USA, Tiffany has put in place a very sophisticated e-learning program. This is necessary if they want to reach many stores at once. Everything is available online. A rigorous structure has been put in place to make sure that every salesperson experiences this self-training tool.*
> (Tiffany shop manager)

Beyond the structural element, the brand's training department must develop online training programs that include many different approaches, in order to make the training entertaining and fun. When I held interviews with salespeople in Sephora stores, they were keen to show me the e-learning tools that had the highest entertainment potential. Some of them were so well designed that salespeople used the training tool several times voluntarily. When I had a closer look at these heart-winning e-learning tools, they were all very colorful, contained videos, brand creator interviews, were very interactive, included music and sometimes almost appeared to be online games. When I designed an online e-learning tool myself for an exclusive skincare brand at Douglas, they asked me to structure it as a quiz. This encouraged people to complete the entire training program, to memorize content and to reduce the number of mistakes, since attractive prizes could be won if you made zero mistakes. Salespeople love challenges. You can therefore transform your training programs into stimulating competitions. And this works!

However, my encounter with hundreds of salespeople and store managers also revealed that e-learning alone was not the solution. It needs to be used as an additional training tool, especially for new product launches where the salesperson must be the first to know about the product. Many salespeople consider e-learning to be an efficient but dehumanizing training method. They benefit greatly from training sessions that favor team experiences.

> *The way we perceive e-learning tools might also be related to our culture. In the USA, for instance, e-learning is already very common. No one would question its usefulness or consider it dehumanizing. In Latin cultures, I think this is different. Having personal contact with a trainer is very important; a real person standing in front of an audience can transmit a lot more emotion.*

> (Tiffany shop manager)

I personally remain convinced that the real brand experience cannot be transmitted more emotionally and convincingly than by highly passionate people who embody and live the brand, whose eyes are sparkling and who will be able to pass on the fire of their passion! Digital training tools, however, are excellent additional channels, especially when time and geography are an issue.

3.4 Pride-booster: Shine as a digital champion!

The further brands manage to project themselves beyond their stores, the stronger the relationship potential with their own sales force. As we have seen before, brands that stand out generate pride in their salespeople. It is therefore very important for brands to develop a strong identity that can be easily recognized worldwide and that contributes to wide-ranging brand awareness.

Pride can also be stimulated by making salespeople feel that they are the best: market leaders, trendsetters ... always ahead of their time. They want to be modern since they represent the brand they sell to their customers.

So the question is: How can digitalization reinforce the pride salespeople have in their brand?

Hardly any communication or sales channels are more global, wide-ranging and omnipresent than the digital ones. Since these channels have such a wide-ranging visibility, it is even more important for brands to be well represented. Make sure that your corporate website, e-commerce platform, Facebook page, Pinterest site or whatever digital channel you decide to use, is up to date. The customer and salesperson should not get

ILL 19 Salespeople's pride: when your brand shines in omnichannels

(Source: Albert Dessinateur for Michaela Merk)

the impression that you are second rate. If you develop digital channels, they must be of top quality, fully in line with your brand image, entertaining, innovative, full of interesting content, conversant with the latest technology and never less attractive than your competition.

The Lacoste example showed me how proud salespeople can be when the brand's Facebook page has millions of fans and is one of the "most liked" premium brands. When you are visibly popular with customers, this reinforces the bonds salespeople have with the brand. So, if you work on your popularity, you will see that this translates immediately in terms of sales force loyalty.

Salespeople also feel extremely proud of their brand when the press talks about it. This gives them the sense of working for a brand of global interest, a brand of fame, a star! When does the press talk about a brand in the digital age? Usually when it is among the first to use a new technology, when its stores are equipped with new digital devices, when a communication campaign is released with tremendous success through social media. In order to do this, you must be daring, you must be ready to take some risks, since being a trendsetter also means that you are venturing into unknown waters. Yet only those who are first can become leaders and garner global press coverage.

Burberry can definitely count itself among the brands that have managed to become a global luxury trendsetter in digital retail management. With their digital flagship store in London, the entire luxury industry, full of both admiration and envy, has its eyes on the British brand. Under the former guidance of Angela Ahrendts and her Chief Creative Officer, Christopher Bailey, the brand has become the digital trendsetter in retail among luxury brands. The impact of such an innovative strength on salespeople is huge. They know that working for Burberry means working for a modern, innovative trendsetter that sets the new digital standards for the fashion industry.

Digital pride can also be generated if you manage to organize events that generate interest in social media or events that your marketing department uses to generate buzz. The more buzz your brand can generate, the higher the relationship-building potential with your sales force.

We organized a pop-up store in the Galeries Lafayette, Paris, for two months during the Christmas period. This kind of temporary store was announced on Facebook, Twitter and on our website. The store was a huge success, and during this period our online sales literally exploded.

(Fred sales associate)

Another great way of allowing your brands to have impact beyond your physical store is to create pop-up stores at huge public events with important media coverage. In the past, products had to be shipped from the warehouse to the temporary store, and storage space needed to be found since it was impossible to know how many people would show up. Today, digital tools can help with sophisticated inventory programs.

Many brands ask for our assistance to help them solve their store retail challenges. For instance, clients may want to set up a pop-up shop at a special event. In this case, they cannot carry the full breadth and depth of the product assortment in these small shops, which leads to stockouts and limits their ability to maximize revenue.

By using Demandware's Digital Store Solution, store associates can place orders for customers against web inventory on a tablet device, thereby making the sale. The products in the warehouse are always accessible, and the goods are shipped to the customer's address.

This solution has significant benefits. First, customers will have increased satisfaction because the store can fulfill their purchase desires. Second, the store converts the lost sale into a real sale, maximizing revenue. And third, the web inventory is faster, freeing up the merchant's option to acquire new products.

(Lawrence Grodzicki, Product Management Director at Demandware, former E-commerce Project Manager and Retail Systems Expert at Timberland)

If your brand operates omnichannels, pride can also arise among salespeople when you start developing products for exclusive online sales.

When we launched our Kate Moss Collection, it included one exclusive product that had been created only for online sales. It was a finger ring

that was made out of silver with black diamonds instead of being made
out of gold with white diamonds. The buzz was huge!

(Fred sales associate)

3.5   Recognition-booster: Better service, digitally!

Heart-winner 15 illustrated that no salesperson's heart could be won without recognition. The recognition expressed by the customer clearly has the strongest impact. If a brand is able to provide its sales force with clever tools to win the customer's heart – such as innovative products presented through convincing sales rituals with a high service potential – salespeople would think twice before leaving their position and joining the competition. The question we need to ask is: How can the digital world help salespeople improve their service level in order to increase their chances of obtaining sincere recognition from their customers?

One digital tool that positively impacts and modifies a salesperson's way to sell is the tablet. I believe that the tablet will become a permanent and indispensable companion to every salesperson since it makes their life so much easier, improves the service level and increases the sales potential for luxury products.

First of all, it is a great tool with which to present the entire product catalogue to customers. In a physical store, space is always limited and an entire collection cannot be exhibited. However, we know how hard it is to sell products that are not openly merchandized. This problem occurs most often with bulky objects such as furniture. Thanks to the tablets, salespeople are now able to show all available and non-available products. They can highlight their explanations with videos and pedagogical graphics. In fashion, they can illustrate the way products are worn using fashion shows as examples. In cosmetics, they can explain the efficiency of products by accessing scientific results conducted on skin, by using images that show the "before" and the "after" result, or by sharing research testimonials. For furniture, videos can show which materials and colors are available to the customer or how a cupboard can be set up and used. This is why Hermès equipped its sales force with tablets at the Paris flagship store since it was impossible to put the entire home collection on display. With the iPad, the problem is solved and salespeople can show their customers whatever design the brand has to offer, even if it is not physically present in the store.

A former sales associate of the famous dancing shoe brand, Repetto, became particularly enthusiastic when I asked him about tablets:

> *I always said that we needed tablets. When a lot of people are in the store and want to be served, we could show them videos about dancing, ballets, and techniques, just to get them in the mood. For kids, we could select a funny ballet, for instance.*
>
> *For professionals, we offered the service of producing tailor-made ballet shoes. We needed to get all the measurements right to ensure the perfect fit. But it was so much more complicated to write all these measurements down on paper than to type them directly into an iPad application. These measurements could then have been transmitted immediately to the production site. This would have allowed us to gain time and be perceived as a modern brand.*

This shows us that tablets can also be helpful devices with regard to tailor-made product services. Why not have the customer create his personal masterpiece after conducting a detailed analysis of needs, wishes and imagination? It is still quite rare, but some brands in high-end watchmaking are using tablets to build the customer's dream watch.

> *When customers don't quite know what they might like, we use our watch configurator iPad application. It allows us to combine the color of the frame with the bracelet and all the details that make a watch so special. For me it is an excellent tool to accompany customers in their selection process. Yet it clearly does not replace us or generate sales on its own.*
>
> (Assistant store manager and after-sales services manager
> at a high-end watchmaking brand)

Many agencies are currently working on applications that optimize a salesperson's daily work.

We have developed an iPad application that will allow the salespeople to stay with their customers throughout the sales process. We have realized how important this is in the high-end jewelry industry, for instance, to never leave your customer alone. Any minor interruption can disturb the customer and take him out of his dream, back to reality, and end the sales conversation. We wanted salespeople to have all information at hand on one device so that they would never have to leave the customer during the highly delicate process of a potential sale. As soon as the customer chooses the product he wants, iPads can be used to signal the need in order to bring the final product out of the storage area to the store, which, in high-end jewelry, is often the stockist's role. In the meantime, the salesperson can remain with the customer, provide him with more details, tell stories about the brand, and inform him of other related products that match the chosen one.

Payment is another moment of truth. In luxury, it is a vulnerable moment. It is therefore important to make this step as smooth as possible. In the USA, it is already quite common to connect your iPad to little devices that allow you to use the iPad or even the iPhone as a cash desk. One of the most developed technologies is called 'square.' Even at the moment of payment, the customer doesn't need to stand up and go to the cash desk. He can remain seated with his salesperson and pay smoothly without queuing. This little device is the beginning of the end for cash desks.

(Pierre Laromiguière, President of Baobaz, web-marketing agency)

Talking about stock: if brands have developed IT systems that control stock levels in all their stores around the world, iPads can be very efficient tools to share stock information.

We recently introduced the iPad in our stores. It is amazing! The iPad indicates in real time if the product is available in-house. If not, the device shows us where the stock can be ordered: in Europe or directly from our central warehouse in Italy. This avoids contacting the head office for questions, which need to be answered immediately if we want to serve our customer in the best way. When using the iPad, we gain time and are able to show the entire catalogue to our customers without fearing that the product they like won't be available.

(Fendi sales associate)

Besides tablets, smart- and iPhones can also increase a salesperson's service options. Interactions with customers become fluid and instantaneous. The process can start before the customer enters the store and can continue once s/he has left. The service sphere is much broader, since it penetrates both the online and offline worlds.

Presenting new collections to our customers at a distance will become so much easier. If a customer wants to see what a dress looks like and cannot come to our boutique herself, someone from our team can wear it, we take a picture with our smartphones and send it to her. We can also do the same with customers we know very well to whom we can proactively send images of new collections assuming that they might like this.

(Shayda de Bary, Store Manager at Sonia Rykiel)

Another idea would be to set up Twitter accounts for customers so that they can communicate instantaneously with the entire sales force as soon as they enter the store. It is quite annoying, especially during commercially busy times, to have to chase after an available sales advisor in a large store, if staff members are all busy or out of reach. Why not link the tweets that customers send in-store to the sale assistants' iPhones or iPads so that they are alerted when someone needs help? The customer might send a message such as, "I need your help. Could someone assist me in choosing an item?" Or, "I am in the dressing room and just tried something on. Could someone bring me another size?" The first available salesperson would come directly to the right spot thanks to geolocalization techniques. In this way, service could be made more reactive, time-saving and transparent thanks to the use of iPhones and access to a Twitter account.

In addition, the salesperson could check in on the geolocalization device Foursquare in order to find out where else the customer shops.

As soon as the customer enters the store, salespeople will be able to know if the person has already bought something in this store, if he has been shopping in my e-boutique and if he is fan of my Facebook page. The aim

ILL 20   **Instore tweets**

(Source: Albert Dessinateur for Michaela Merk)

> *is to create a virtual process in order to design a tailor-made one-on-one customer purchasing experience. This is the future of shopping.*
>
> (Christian Radmilovitch, Digital Expert and Consultant)

Besides sending photos to customers, you could also direct them to a visual merchandising department. With this in place, sharing best practices between employees can become much easier, and more accurate and fluid, across the globe. Pictures of beautiful installations in a shop window can become benchmarks for other sales teams. If previous products need to be displayed, there would be a perfect reference available. Service would, consequently, be improved within departments. In order to make things even better, each department should think of ways to improve its service level in relation to other departments.

Service is perceived as service once customer expectations are met, anticipated or even exceeded. This requires a perfect knowledge of their habits, needs and desires. To do so, data collection, analysis and availability are crucial. Once again, the digital world provides sophisticated solutions that enable retailers and brands to know their customers better. The challenge is to provide tools for salespeople, who are on the front line, enabling them to identify the profile of their customer from the very beginning of their interaction. These tools enable them to provide a better service, create higher customer satisfaction and obtain stronger customer recognition. And this, we know, strengthens the bonds between salespeople and their brand.

iPhone or iTouch applications are increasingly emerging, allowing sales advisors to have all existing customer data on hand. Thanks to a highly profiled database, the cosmetics retailer Sephora has developed an iTouch application for its sales force:

> The application 'My Sephora' allows salespeople to access a large customer base by simply scanning the customer's loyalty card or by typing the loyalty card number. With this device, salespeople have access to all customer-related data, they can see what the last purchases were, the customer's preferences and his spending power, and can therefore provide a personalized service. They can also offer relevant promotional activities or offer better advice thanks to videos such as product tutorials. On the other hand, Sephora developed an application for customers, who can view customer-to-customer recommendations and comments from the entire community. Sephora is very innovative in this respect, trying to move forward in sales force and customer relationship management by providing digital tools for salespeople and customers.
>
> (Christian Radmilovitch, Digital Expert and Consultant)

Profiled customer data also allows salespeople to interact more closely and frequently with their clients. Today, VIP customers even expect their preferred brand to offer them a privileged space online, which allows them to interact directly with their personal sales advisor.

> More and more luxury customers are keen on having their personal space on the brand's online site, in order to be able to ask questions at any moment or under any circumstances: 'I damaged my Louis Vuitton handbag, what can I do? I will spend three days in Hong Kong, can you give me advice on the best outfit to wear?' It is very gratifying for salespeople to be seen as an advisor rather than a simple salesperson. This is what creates recognition and strengthens salespeople's bonds with their brands.
>
> (Jean-Charles Champey, former Retail Operations Director at Miu Miu)

Training is required to use these digital devices, which are increasingly becoming salespeople's companions and service assistants. During training sessions, salespeople should gain a better technical understanding of the devices, and should also learn how to use these in interaction with the customer. It is important to avoid situations where salespeople are so focused on their iPads that they forget to concentrate on the customer. I have seen salespeople fail to greet their clients because they were too focused on their touch screens, which they manipulated in the middle of the store. The selling ritual with digital devices will change. Each industry segment makes best use of iPads and smartphones in different ways, which should be worked out in cooperation with experts. The tools as such are great, but the rules must be clearly defined. Otherwise, the service level will not increase but considerably decrease, and customer relationships will get more and more dehumanized. This is the opposite of what we want.

In order to integrate digital devices more easily into existing sales rituals, the newly designed devices for salespeople are getting smaller and smaller. Several digital companies are currently designing multifunctional tools that provide everything salespeople need to accompany their customers throughout the sales process: from barcode scan, to payment facilities, to access to customer data, to the inventory and the online shop. Such a device is only slightly larger than an iPhone, and can be combined with an iPad if you want to make impactful product demonstrations.

In order to gain maximum support from the sales teams, organizing brainstorming sessions such as "how to use iPads and smartphones in the store" could be interesting. Such brainstorming sessions could help salespeople identify with their new devices, and give them the feeling of having contributed to the modernization of the brand. Why not choose one store as your pioneer location to test and implement the digital sales ritual, under the guidance of a digital retail expert, before deploying the new approach throughout the rest of your retail environment? In the deployment process, you may even spot some digital savvy salespeople who could help train other salespeople or establish comprehensive hands-on training tools. Once again, this could be a great opportunity for your sales teams to gain tremendous recognition.

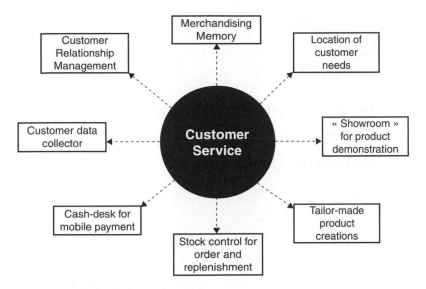

FIG 24 / **The digital service carousel**

How Brands Can Benefit from Strong Sales Force–Brand Relationships

Why should companies try their best to win salespeople's hearts?

Why should companies do everything they can to:

- kindle salespeople's love for their brand
- facilitate their brand identification
- reinforce their trust in the brand they are selling
- stir up their pride in the brand
- and enhance the recognition they might receive from customers, managers or colleagues?

In this chapter you will find the answers.

4.1 Emotional explosion: The boomerang effect of motivation

Meeting and holding discussions with so many salespeople across various luxury sectors allowed me to collect plenty of data that clearly showed how greatly strong sales force–brand relationships contribute to employee motivation. The scientific analyses I conducted over the course of my doctorate thesis using this data confirmed this assumption.

Motivation, again, is a very important aspect of people management since it has an incredible influence over a company's success. It could be compared to the fuel that brings a car to high speed, the wind that lifts the kite high into the air, the fire that fills a cold room with heat. It is the engine for higher achievements. Without your people's motivation, nothing happens.

Other attempts to capture the power of motivation have been made by C. C. Pinder, who defines work motivation as "a set of energetic forces that originates both from within as well as beyond an individual's being, to initiate work-related behavior, and to determine its form, direction, intensity, and duration."[1] In other words, work motivation is the energy that stimulates people to accomplish their work. It influences their decisions relating to task achievement and determines how much effort people invest in trying, and why they stop trying. According to S. Robbins, motivation represents the "willingness to exert high levels of effort toward organizational goals, conditioned by the effort's ability to satisfy some individual needs."[2]

These energies allow salespeople to go beyond their capacities, to do more than requested or expected. They do it naturally without feeling it to be an additional burden or effort.

> *You are simply willing to give more than 100 percent. You also believe in what you say and you fully unite with your brand. When you talk about your brand, it is almost as if you were talking about a family member. It all becomes so natural. And it is this natural aspect that is very convincing and makes customers buy.*
>
> (Repetto sales associate)

> *I was so passionate about our brand that I continued to work during breaks. I started creating mood boards on our competitors or I sorted out which products looked best together, in order to display the items in the most attractive way.*
>
> (Store manager at a luxury shoe brand)

> *Motivation expresses itself directly through the degree of implication. As a store manager, I fixed a very ambitious objective for the entire team: on the first day of the sales period I wanted to do the best sellout that*

[1] C. C. Pinder (1998) *Motivation in Work Organizations*. Upper Saddle River, NY: Prentice Hall.
[2] S. Robbins (1993) *Organizational Behavior* (6th edn.). Englewood Cliffs, NJ: Prentice Hall.

had ever been achieved since our store opening seven years ago. At 8 am everyone was present in their starting blocks, ready to give their best. Although people should have worked in shifts from 8 am to 3 pm and from 3 pm to 10 pm, they all stayed and worked the entire day. They didn't even find the time to have a decent lunch break. So we bought a large sushi platter and put it in the backroom of our boutique in order to replenish their stomach. There was one salesperson who was pregnant and I had to force her not to work from 8 am to 10 pm, non-stop, like everyone else. All that incredible commitment paid off and we achieved the best sales figure in our store history.

(Store manager at a luxury fashion brand)

Besides going above and beyond their daily tasks, motivated salespeople provide better service. They are keen to suggest their brand, talk about it, share its secrets and sell it. And they do it all with a big smile on their face.

Motivation also stimulates communication, the willingness to share and to transmit information. When sales teams are motivated, they communicate among each other, they exchange easily with their manager and their customers.

As floor manager, I created a welcome booklet for the new salespeople in my team. It contained information about our brand, the products, the company structure. I handed it out to trainees, new arrivals or anyone who had to be initiated into the brand. It was important to have a document at hand to explain all procedures, our store, the brand, the bestsellers and how to read the references. No one asked me to do that, but I felt keen to do it for our brand. Then I started welcome training in the morning before the store opened.

(Store manager at a luxury fashion brand)

Finally, all salespeople agree that motivation sells. The more a team is motivated, the stronger their personal investment and the higher the sales of the store. Highly motivated teams are the best brand ambassadors.

Besides identifying the motivational power of strong sales force–brand relationships, I observed another interesting phenomenon: the boomerang effect of motivation. As we all know, a boomerang is a piece of hard wood that comes back to the person who threw it into the air. The energy of motivation also seems to come back to the person who released it. I observed this at various levels of interaction in the field: between the store manager and the sales assistants, among sales assistants, and between the sales force and their customers. The first person to initially throw the boomerang of motivation is usually the store manager. His or her role is decisive in the motivation-building process.

> *Managers are at the heart of the store and their role is to transmit their enthusiasm to their teams. When we are motivated, we are willing to move faster, we are filled with energy to work more and we want to pass this energy on to our teams. This immediately translates into positive sales results for the store. When I see that my sales associates are as motivated as I am, my energy level rises even higher. It's a great feeling that you simply want to hold, repeat and pass on.*
>
> (Sephora store manager)

The energy of motivation from a manager to a salesperson can spill over to the latter's colleagues. A highly motivated salesperson has a great capacity to transmit his energy to other salespeople, which encourages a good team spirit and usually generates positive sales figures.

The third level of motivation spillover happens when salespeople interact with their customers.

> *When I see that my customers are highly satisfied with a brand or product I sold to them, I feel incredibly happy. But it's only when a product truly convinces me that I can pass on my enthusiasm naturally and honestly.*
>
> (Sephora sales advisor)

This amplifying effect on all three levels is extremely powerful and can considerably impact the success of a point of sale.

Just as motivation has a positive spillover effect on others, one person's lack of motivation within the team can be disastrous, since it can affect the motivation of others. Unmotivated people must be carefully monitored and, if necessary, removed from the sales environment, as they can cause a lot of damage. It is particularly bad when these people interact directly with customers, since they are likely to talk negatively about the brand.

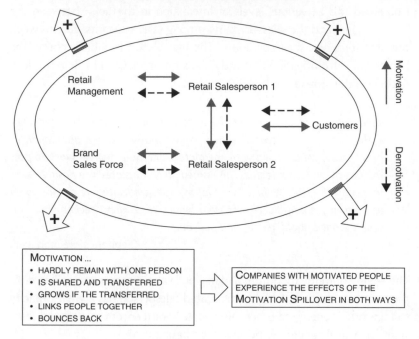

THE SYSTEM OF MOTIVATION-SPILLOVER

FIG 25 / The boomerang effect of motivation

The model below illustrates how the spillover effect of motivation develops in a retail environment at all store levels: with managers, salespeople and customers. The flashes in both directions indicate that motivation hardly ever remains within one person but is shared and transferred. Motivation grows as soon as the transfer happens. It links people together and bounces back as a boomerang with even more positive energy (Figure 25).

All these chain reactions occur when as a brand has managed to establish strong relationships with its salespeople.

4.2 Organizational commitment: Your sales force will stay!

When your salespeople have established close relationships with your brand, they are not only spreading their positive energy throughout and beyond your brand, but they are also willing to remain with the company. The scientific term is "organizational commitment."

D. T. Hall and H. T. Nygren viewed commitment as a state in which individuals' identification with an organization and its corporate goals is so strong that they wish to remain a member of this organization in order to contribute to the achievement of its goals.[3] L. W. Porter, W. J. Crampon and F. W. Smith define commitment as the intensity of a person's identification with and involvement in a particular organization.[4] Commitment is seen as a binding force that adds stability to a relationship over time.[5]

Scientists who analyzed organizational commitment found that employees remained loyal to their firm, brand or company for three main reasons: emotions, costs or norms.

Affective organizational commitment is the result of an emotional attachment to the organization. It can be defined as "the attachment of an individual's fund of affectivity and emotion to the group."[6] It is the result of shared values and identification. This is the type of attachment I am looking at in this book, since brand relationships are based on emotions.

The second type of commitment is called continuance organizational commitment and is the result of perceived costs related to the eventual termination of a job. Employees often accumulate interesting "side bets" such as pensions, social security and other comfortable bonuses.[7] By leaving the organization, they would lose these bonuses and they recognize the cost associated with this action. Furthermore, a lack of alternative employment could also be a motive to stay loyal to the original

---

[3] D. T. Hall and H. T. Nygren (1970) "Personal factors in organization identification." *Administrative Science Quarterly*, 15, 176–89.

[4] L. W. Porter, W. J. Crampon and F. W. Smith (1976) "Organizational commitment and managerial turnover: a longitudinal study." *Organizational Behavior and Human Performance*, 15, 87–98.

[5] C. E. Rusbult (1983) "A longitudinal test of the investment model: the development (and deterioration) of satisfaction and commitment in heterosexual involvements." *Journal of Personality and Social Psychology*, 45(1), 101–17.

[6] R. M. Kanter (1968) "Commitment and social organization: a study of commitment mechanisms in utopian communities." *American Sociological Review*, 33, 499–517.

[7] H. S. Becker (1960) "Notes on the concept of commitment." *American Journal of Sociology*, 66, 32–40.

organization.[8] A contract is one of the main mechanisms that limits employees in their search for alternatives, and often generates switching costs when they leave the organization.

The third type of commitment is called normative organizational commitment and refers to an individual who "considers it morally right to stay in the company, regardless of how much status enhancement or satisfaction the firm gives him over the years."[9] Such feelings of obligation are like "normative pressures to act in a way, which meets organizational goals and interests."[10]

In sum, some employees with strong affective commitment traits will stay loyal to their company because they are emotionally attached to it.

Then there are those who feel that leaving their employer would be too costly and decide to stay because they need to do so.

And others might feel pressured to remain within the organization because it is a moral obligation.

Organizational commitment plays a crucial role in a company's success, since it addresses the challenge of keeping employees committed and loyal to their organization.

> When Apple established itself in France, it was very hard to headhunt their salespeople since they felt extremely committed to their brand. This was especially linked to the fact that they had undergone excellent training and integration programs. To me, this example is a real benchmark of organizational commitment.
>
> (Eric Egiziano, Headhunter at Lincoln Associates)

Existing sales management literature has shown that salespeople are an organization's key asset. Maintaining the commitment salespeople have toward the organization is one of the biggest challenges companies face

---

[8] J. P. Meyer and N. J. Allen (1991) "A three-component conceptualization of organizational commitment." *Human Resource Management Review*, 1(1), 61–89.

[9] J. G. Marsh and H. Mannari (1977) "Organizational commitment and turnover: a predictive study." *Administrative Science Quarterly*, 22, 57–75.

[10] Y. Wiener (1982) "Commitment to organizations: a normative view." *Academy of Management Review*, 7, 418–28.

today.[11] The personal implications for an employee who has developed a form of organizational commitment can go far beyond actual professional tasks,[12] since it might lead to their willingness to:

- make personal sacrifices for the organization
- make efforts without receiving rewards
- show personal preoccupation for the organization.

> *The prestige that surrounds luxury brands generates strong admiration, pride and passion, animating salespeople in their daily interactions with the product and the client. Even though some very famous brands don't pay a high salary, salespeople still dream of working for them. They are ready to make financial sacrifices just to be able to work for famous international luxury brands and get widespread social recognition. When you work in luxury, you get used to the luxury codes. Someone who drives a beautiful car but works in an unknown place might prefer working for Vuitton as a manager and riding a simple bike. This might, among other factors, derive from the fact that he feels proud to say that he works for Louis Vuitton whenever people ask him about his workplace. This pride of belonging is huge. Brands like Chanel, Dior, Van Cleef & Arpels make salespeople dream just because of their tremendous international and prestigious fame. So does Place Vendôme, where the most prestigious watches and jewelry brands are based.*
>
> *Since we have realized how important it is to have a strong name in order to keep your sales force, we are also working on the brand awareness of the name Printemps. One of our competitors opened a new store not very far away from ours. Their human resources department approached some of our best salespeople, offering them a 25 percent increase in salary. Even though the salaries of salespeople at Printemps are not very high, they*

---

[11] E. Anderson and T. S. Robertson (1995) "Inducing multiline salespeople to adopt house brands." *Journal of Marketing*, 59 (April), 16–31.
[12] L. B. Chonko (1986) "Organizational commitment in the sales force." *Journal of Personal Selling and Management*, 6, 19–27.

> *remained with us. They identify so strongly with our house that no monetary sum could convince them to leave. This is especially true for people who had been working here for a long time. The ones who decided to leave were mostly young salespeople, whose relationship with our brand was not very solid or established.*
>
> (Alexandre Ferragu, former Retail Sales Manager
> Luxury and Accessories at Printemps)

Commitment to your organization grows over time. The longer salespeople relate to their brand, suggest others purchase its products and are daily in its environment, the tighter their hearts will be tied to their brand. They become inseparable, like best friends or even a passionate couple. They want each other, they need each other. Leaving is not an option. Even thinking about it seems impossible. Whenever I asked highly committed salespeople about the option of working for their brand's competitor, they looked at me as if this was the most idiotic question I could ask. Many strongly committed salespeople had been serving their brand for a long time, sometimes ten, twenty or even thirty years. The amount of love and passion they feel for their brand is immense. So is their level of trust and their identification with it. Their pride could be sensed in each word they uttered about their brand. This was also the case when they interacted with their colleagues and clients. After so many years, they have become true ambassadors who embody the brand completely. In most cases, they have established a solid relationship not only with their brand but also with their customers. While salespeople who have the strongest organizational commitment are extremely loyal to their company – their own customers are extremely loyal to them. Committed salespeople end up knowing every single detail about their brand and their customers. That is how they reinforce ties and strengthen relationships over time.

Recruitment Strategies for Strong Sales Force–Brand Relationships

There are many "first" steps in recruitment: the first interview, the first impression, the trial period.

Recruiting salespeople with a strong relationship potential is similar to love at first sight. It happens when a man and a woman meet for the first time and have the feeling that they are made for each other, that they are willing to share more, that they want to comfort and support each other. It is an intense emotional moment.

In a recruitment process where finding people who have lasting relationship potential matters, emotion plays a predominant role, much more so than knowledge or education. The challenge for recruiters is to feel the heartbeat, to identify the burning fire within.

> *There are people who see their professional relationship as similar to being engaged in a couple. It is extraordinary to find these kinds of people, since they stay loyal through tough times, thanks to their passion. It has a lot to do with someone's attitude, personal goals, character, his past and his dreams. To be honest with you, I meet fewer and fewer juniors who embody this attitude. The more senior people are the ones who still have this intense perception of loyalty.*
>
> (Eric Egiziano, Headhunter at Lincoln Associates)

After having identified the heart-winners that allow a brand to establish closer and longer-lasting bonds with its sales force, I want to outline how to find heart-winning salespeople. My goal in this chapter is to help human resources, brand, retail and general managers to identify relationship potential by noticing the right indicators, and asking the right questions. Finding the best-fitting people, especially in sales, is not an easy task. But it is essential in order to protect and develop your brand on a long-term basis. It is therefore advisable to sometimes wait instead of recruiting the wrong candidate, who could be damaging for your brand and your team.

5.1   Finding people who can light the fire and inspire

In order to find people who can light the fire, we need the right elements and foundation. No fire can burn if you do not use the right wood or charcoal and if you do not place them all in such a way that the flame will ignite and last. During the recruitment process, you should be looking for exactly the same thing. True passion cannot be identified if those who select the candidates are not filled with passion themselves. The hearts of the recruiters must burn for the brand in order to see and feel heart-winning potential.

Once this fundamental condition is fulfilled you can start to determine which candidates have the right personalities for each role. This approach is threefold: it requires you to have the capacity to observe physical and verbal elements as well as the courage to listen to your intuition.

1 – Physical expression

The most important physical expression is a smile. Smiling is the key heart-winning expression for all successful salespeople. A welcoming warmhearted smile is worth more than millions of words. It is the most universal sign of positive exchange, attention and sympathy. A smile has something energetic to it. You can feel the positive energy in people by the way they are smiling. What we are looking for is the true, honest smile, not the artificial, crispy, "I must smile to look friendly" type. There are people who have real trouble smiling naturally. They will probably have a hard time becoming successful.

> *When I hire someone, I always look at their natural service attitude. But even more importantly, I want to see if they can smile. If a candidate doesn't smile at me during the entire interview, I consider that the person*

ILL 21 Fire-detector strategy for recruitment

(Source: Albert Dessinateur for Michaela Merk)

is not fit for working in a service-related industry. Smiling is important but can hardly be trained.

(Verena Lasvigne, Senior Spa Director at Four Seasons Hotels and Resorts)

Besides a warmhearted smile, the expression in people's eyes can also give a clear sign as to their personality. Eyes should sparkle whenever potential salespeople talk about something they love doing.

When you recruit your salespeople, you need to look into their eyes. This is where you can see what is really going on inside. Don't make the mistake of only talking about business. Make sure

> *that you ask potential recruits about their lives, hobbies, sports, and politics. This is when they really start revealing themselves since, during the rest of the interview process, they are usually so keen to impress that they perform. You can't see a true person immediately. As soon as they relax, however, you can identify who are the lazy aristocrats, the aggressive worriers or those who will make your life difficult since they want to be the boss. What I want are passionate warriors who have the power and enthusiasm to fight for the brand. In order to see what the candidate is really like, you need to be sure to look at the professional performance and results but also at all the personal aspects. Then you can finalize your judgment by looking in their eyes.*
>
> (Alain Dominique Perrin, Non-Executive Director at Richemont Group,
> former President of Cartier International,
> President of EFMD (European Foundation for Management Development)
> and President of EDC (École des Dirigeants et Créateurs d'Entreprises))

Together with the facial expressions comes posture and gestures. Winning gestures in the sales process serve to clarify and underline a message rather than disturb the customer. Gestures can also calm the customer during a "stressful" decision-making process, which involves spending a lot of money to purchase a luxury item. Gestures in sales need to be balanced, harmonious, positive, and should never be hectic or intimidating. Yet, in order to convey competence, your candidates should express confidence in their overall attitude: standing straight but not being stiff, pulling shoulders back instead of hunching them, keeping the head straight without constantly looking down or avoiding direct eye contact.

Questions recruiters should ask themselves while observing the candidate:

- Is the candidate smiling easily?
- Is the smile natural or artificial?
- What is the smile expressing: sympathy, passion, joy or rather embarrassment?
- What can I read in the eyes of my candidate: are they sparkling out of motivation or filled with fear?

- Does the candidate look into my eyes when s/he is talking, and/or when I am talking?
- Which impression did I get when the candidate walked into the room?
- How did the handshake feel?
- Does the person convey confidence and self-assurance?
- How was the candidate sitting in front of you? Look at the posture, the position of the legs and arms.
- What are the person's gestures like: hectic or harmonious, winning or stressful, convincing or confusing?
- Is the person's physical appearance in line with luxury standards (Are their shoes polished? Is their tie properly tied? Is their outfit clean and tidy? Are their nails well maintained? Etc.)

The main aim of these questions is to detect true passion for the sales position you are offering and for your brand through the candidate's body language. The candidate should convey confidence and harmony and have a winning personality, judging from the way he or she looks, smiles, walks and behaves.

2 – Verbal content

While certain heart-winning character traits can be identified through simply looking, your observations need to be completed by assessing verbal content. Which areas are important to analyze in order to find the candidate who has strong relationship potential?

1. Check out what animates the candidate: Money or the brand!

Is the person's first motivation to earn money or a passionate desire to serve your brand? If you get the impression that money is the predominant motivation to take up a sales job, this is a bad sign for a lasting relationship. Make sure that the person applies out of a true interest for the brand and has a desire to sell it. In order to find out about their motivation, you can ask a series of targeted questions, but you can also find out by the way the candidates have prepared their interview. Don't simply judge on good interview preparation though – make sure that the interest is natural. Therefore, carefully observe the way they talk about your brand, paying attention to words coupled with physical expressions.

You can easily identify why candidates apply by analyzing the type of questions they ask. If one of the first questions is to know more about the compensation system, especially the commission, I know that the person is mainly applying to make money and not out of love for the brand. Those who apply out of passion ask questions indicating that they want to better understand the required tasks: How do I participate in the purchasing process? How am I involved in the selection process of new products? Can I give some input when it comes to merchandising in the store?

(Sylvie Coumau, General Manager of Editions de Parfums Frédéric Malle)

As a retail operations manager, when going through the recruitment process, I try to understand if the potential salesperson applied because he saw a great opportunity to earn money or if the application is really driven by true passion. I quite often encounter salespeople who are only looking for a great source of income and prestige. Since there is a rising amount of international luxury shoppers, multicultural salespeople are very much sought after in the market. Therefore, these candidates chase the highest revenue possible. They are willing to work for any kind of brand just to make money and get commissions. And then there are the others who apply because they want to realize a dream and work for a luxury brand they feel close to. The name Miuccia Prada, for instance, fills them with enthusiasm. In this case, they are willing to accept a lot just to be able to work for their preferred brand. It's only with these types of people that you can really build a lasting relationship in the long run without having them jumping from one brand to another, chasing the best salary. One of the things that indicates true interest for the brand is the way candidates prepare for the interview. If they know the creative director's name, the brand history, the role of Miu Miu within our Group, if they watched the latest fashion shows, are informed about the products, visited a store, talked to sales advisors and are able to paint a picture of the brand within the fashion environment, they usually want the job out of passion. If they only looked at our website a few times, their knowledge of the brand is usually not very extensive.

(Jean-Charles Champey, former Retail Operations Director at Miu Miu)

Questions to ask during the interview:

- Why did you decide to apply for this job?
- What motivated you to contact us?
- What do you expect from this position?
- What do you think and know about our brand?
- Have you ever been in our stores? If yes, when was it and what was your general impression?
- How do you see our brand compared to its competitors?
- Why do you think you could fit with our brand?

These questions should enable you to discover your candidates' true motivation: Did they apply to earn money or to serve your brand? Pay attention to their need to work for financial reasons. Is it really the brand that attracts them rather than the money?

2. Check your candidate's true interest in the customer

Good salespeople are fully connected with their brand but should also connect with their customers. One of the errors in recruitment is that brands sometimes focus exclusively on the candidate's compatibility with the brand instead of testing the person's true interest in the customer.

> *I often get a preselection of great-looking, stylish salespeople. But many times I discover that they totally lack interest in our customers. Our best salespeople and store managers are not necessarily the best-looking ones. However, they have developed real relationships with their customers. Understanding their needs and dreams animates them. Certainly, an attractive look is also important, but it should not be the decisive criteria. Especially in an economic crisis, which we are currently facing, custom-ers are more willing to make a compromise on salesperson style than on service quality.*

(Elisabeth Cazorla, President of Jacadi)

Customer focus is even more important at times when there needs to be a real differentiation in service between stores and digital sales channels. Therefore, testing the customer–brand relationship potential should be a key element in your recruitment process.

In order to test a salesperson's true customer-relationship potential, you need to assess their natural level of generosity and their people-loving capacity. Being generous means being willing to give in order to receive.

> *It is impossible to grow beautiful flowers if you haven't prepared your soil and if you haven't irrigated them properly.*
> (Alain Dominique Perrin, Non-Executive Director at Richemont Group,
> former President of Cartier International,
> President of EFMD (European Foundation for Management Development)
> and President of EDC (École des Dirigeants et Créateurs d'Entreprises))

> *Good salespeople love others and are interested in them.*
> (Natalie Bader, CEO of Prada France,
> former President at Fred International and
> former Marketing Director at Sephora)

One of the most efficient ways to discover character traits such as generosity and service sense is to play out real sales situations during the interview. Put your candidate into a scenario that might really happen in a store and observe their reaction. Design simulations in which your candidate is confronted by different customer profiles in order to test his/her empathy, flexibility and spontaneity. Sincere reactions can best be observed in such role-playing games, since they reveal true character.

These character traits are opposed to arrogance, which is the antithesis of a customer-oriented service attitude. For that reason, it is important to detect arrogance in recruitment interviewees.

Questions to ask during the interview:

- How would your friends describe you?
- What does selling mean to you?
- What is your interest in selling?
- Which qualities do you have to become a successful salesperson for our brand?
- What does "service" mean to you?
- Which qualities are counterproductive in the service industry?

Make sure that customer focus and the wish to serve are predominant elements of the candidate's motivation. A sense of generosity and love for others should be clearly visible. Try to sense if arrogance is in the air.

3. Check your candidate's positive attitude

Positive-minded people tend to find it easier to establish lasting relationships than those who permanently raise doubts. They create a favorable environment around them, which is essential when building relationships with colleagues, customers and your brand, and fosters team spirit and customer loyalty. Positive thinkers are important members of your team as they can smooth out tensions, attempt to find solutions when problems arise and are willing to reach out toward new horizons for the brand.

> *A good salesperson is able to think positively. Why not ask the candidate to analyze several sentences you provide in order to test his sensibility in relation to a given topic? Then ask them to interpret the sentence and see if their interpretation leads to a positive or a negative perception.*
> (Paul Bassène, High Jewelry Manager at Cartier)

Questions you could ask during an interview:

- Whenever you are in a difficult situation, what do you do? Give an example from your past.
- What would you do if sales were very low and customers weren't coming into the store?
- Can you think of a situation in which you gave up?

These kinds of question are designed to see if your candidates tend to be positive thinkers and if they are willing to stick with a situation even if it is difficult. Find out if the person would rather give up or if they would do anything in their power to succeed and solve the problem.

4. Check your candidate's level of curiosity

Training is a predominant heart-winner. But in order to make training useful, the salesperson must be willing to learn and to absorb new information. Retaining information also requires that people are willing to train themselves, to know more about the brand and to stay constantly up to date. People who lack curiosity neither memorize information nor are they able to reproduce it. It is therefore important to find candidates who are naturally open-minded, capable of asking questions and eager to stay informed.

> *I see myself as a passionate person with a very good general knowledge of culture. Since I am interested in so many things, I am always open to learning more and I believe I have a very good memory. All this helps me to engage with my customers on topics they wish to discuss: the art of wine tasting, kings and queens, high-fashion brands or any other possible topic.*
>
> (Store manager at a high-end watchmaking brand)

Questions to ask during an interview:

- What are your main fields of interest?
- If you had the unique opportunity to learn more about another area, which one would you chose?
- Have you ever taken a voluntary training course? If so, please give details.
- Which training programs made you grow and made you more marketable?

These questions should allow you to identify the candidates' willingness to learn, to improve themselves and to become better informed on any subject. It's important to find out if your candidate likes to learn, as this will help them to connect with customers on a higher level.

5. Check the intensity of the candidate's bonds with your brand

True passion for a brand may have emerged in early childhood. This may be because parents or close relatives have bought from the brand, talked positively about it, or even given a product from it as a present for a special occasion. People might associate positive feelings with the brand or strong emotions; they may remember unique and happy moments from the past. If you're able to identify a candidate that has formed a natural bond with your brand because of relationships that were established many years ago, there is a strong likelihood that this person will be filled with lasting and true passion while serving the brand as a salesperson.

> *Cartier was the first brand I wanted to work for. This is related to my past. My grandparents loved this brand. Their first watch was Cartier. I gave Cartier's Love Bracelet to my daughter for her 20th birthday. And I gave the*

Must of Cartier watch to my dad for his 60th birthday. I truly love all the stories that are related to this amazing brand, which is filled with history.
(Store manager at a high-end watchmaking and jewelry brand)

Questions you could ask during an interview:

- What links you to the brand?
- When did you first hear about the brand?
- What is the image you have of the brand?
- When did your wish to work for our brand emerge?
- Have you ever purchased one of our brand's products?

These questions allow you to find out if a previous bond with the brand exists or if the candidates have simply answered a job offer they saw on the Internet.

6. Check a person's stability

Salespeople who frequently switch brands are less likely to establish strong, lasting brand relationships. Such people find constant change stimulating. Their passion for one brand might not be strong enough for the bond to be durable. It's only when salespeople stay within a brand for several years that they can experience what it means to build a solid customer base and intense brand relationships. Of course, it is good to find people who have experienced many different brands and worked in multiple retail environments. However, these salespeople will probably not stay with your brand for long. It is not in their genes. Throughout all the interviews I conducted, I noticed that time played an important role in the relationship-building process. The longer salespeople served a brand, the more the brand became part of their lives. Some of them had developed absolute faith in the brand and always defended it to the hilt. They had served customers over the course of generations: the grandparents, the parents and their kids. Their customer bonds and ties with the brand are solid and cannot be easily destroyed.

There are salespeople who have been serving the brand for over twenty years. They know our brand by heart and have developed full trust in the brand. A salesperson must progress and learn over time. I am therefore always very skeptical of salespeople who keep passing from one brand to another. I prefer the ones who are proud of their profession and brand and who love their customers. In the Hermès flagship store at Faubourg Saint-Honoré, you can find salespeople who have known their customers for years. When their clients arrive, they already know exactly what products to suggest because they are very familiar with the customers' tastes, inner wishes and needs.

(Christian Blanckaert, Professor in Luxury Management at ESCP Europe and former CEO of Hermès Sellier and Hermès International)

Questions you could ask during an interview:

- Why have you switched jobs several times in the past?
- In your opinion how long should a salesperson stay in one company and serve the brand?
- What would you do if you felt that you were not progressing anymore?
- Why could it be beneficial for you to stay with one brand for many years?
- Where do you see yourself in five years from now?

These questions should help you find out if your candidates might leave you after a few months, if they gets a more attractive financial offer, or if they see a real benefit in staying and engaging with the brand for a longer period.

7. Check a person's capacity to observe and adapt

Salespeople who can light the fire with passion have a huge potential for empathy and adaptability. They sense changes in an environment or situation by observing and listening, and are able to adapt to suit the new scenario, whether it is a result of changing customer behavior, or due to changes within the brand. We live in a world of constant movement, which requires huge adaptation capacities. Good salespeople need to sense how they can touch their customers' hearts, how they can make them dream, in which ways and circumstances they can suggest products that fully correspond to their customers' inner needs and desires.

I sometimes feel like a chameleon, which is an animal that perfectly reflects my true philosophy as a salesperson. This animal carefully approaches new territories and carefully pays attention to where it puts its feet. It observes a situation from all its angles, looks ahead but also to each side and backwards. It's only when it feels totally secure, when the soil is not too hot, that the chameleon puts its feet on the ground and moves on. If danger is in the air, it hides by adapting its own color to the surrounding area. It becomes invisible to the outside world, while still observing its environment with a 360-degree angle. When everything seems secure again, it moves on in the right direction.

(Paul Bassène, High Jewelry Manager at Cartier)

During the interview, try to discover if the candidate has an aversion to potential change. In many European countries, employees resistant to change are so well protected by law that they can remain in their role and can hurt the well-being and success of a company by spreading a negative attitude. Instead of fostering ties, these salespeople could manage to break them. In your interviews, try to identify the candidate's true attitude toward change, since change will happen!

Questions you could ask during an interview:

- What are the most important characteristics of a good salesperson?
- What quality is fundamental to the sales profession in order to make your customers dream?
- Illustrate your approach when selling a luxury product to a customer.
- What would you do in order to find out what the customer really wants?
- How important is it for a brand to change over time?
- If you were the manager, how would you proceed when implementing major changes in the organization in which the sales force is involved?

These questions should allow you to see whether the candidates consider the observation and understanding of the customer as essential qualities for successful sales. Test their capacity to listen. This can be checked throughout the interview. Do they ask questions or are they constantly talking? You should also find out if your candidates are flexible enough to adapt to changing environments or if they would be the first to complain if habits needed to be modified.

3 – Intuition

People who have strong relationship potential can be identified by observing their physical expressions and by listening to their verbal statements. Yet there is another aspect recruiters should not neglect. Since we want to detect the candidate's emotional capacities, recruiters must be able to listen to their own inner voices. This inner voice, called intuition, must be the last referee to decide upon a "go" or a "no go."

During my interviews with CEOs and top managers, the word "intuition" came up many times.

> *Today, most brands seek security by recruiting people with solid experience in their respective business sectors, for instance in fashion and luxury. But besides the candidates' background and professional profile, intuition is also very important in the recruitment process. I always attempt to imagine potential recruits in our sales environment, trying to see whether they would fit in or not. I try to assess how the candidates might interact with others, how they behave when they communicate with customers and how they sell.*
>
> (Elodie Leprince-Ringuet, International Retail Director at Robert Clergerie, former European Retail Director at Bonpoint)

> *In the field of luxury especially, it is the recruiters' role to find people whose eyes sparkle due to passion for the brand. The selection process must not only be driven by rational thoughts but by intuition. Recruiters should find this relatively easy since they are already living the brand from within, a brand filled with emotions and dreams. It's a lot about our hearts.*
>
> (Agnès Combes, Training Director at Chanel, former International Training Director at Guerlain)

5.2   Matching origins and values

The heart-winning strategies, in particular heart-winners 2 and 4, showed how important it is for brands to allow salespeople to literally dive into the brand's universe. When salespeople fully understand your values, they are able to love the brand and identify with it. We have also seen that a mismatch between the salesperson's values and the brand's values can cause dissatisfaction or even a major rupture.

During the recruitment process, it is therefore crucial to determine if these values are identical. Be sure to ask the candidates about their perception of the brand, the brand values that they appreciate most, the values they seem to have in common with the brand. Try to analyze the gap between your brand reality from the corporate point of view and the candidate's brand perception.

Find out what the overlaps and the differences are, in order to judge compatibility.

Since it is difficult to gain a fully accurate perception of values during a one- or two-hour interview, the first three- to six-month trial period on the job is essential. It gives recruiters a chance to double-check their impressions during the interview and to validate the candidate.

> *I feel that the trial period is very important. A person who left a very good impression in the first interviews but showed a lack of willingness to invest energy in daily tasks would probably not pass this period. But these attitudes are hard to detect during a simple discussion. You definitely need to see how the person behaves in the store.*
> (Jean-Charles Champey, former Retail Operations Director at Miu Miu)

My series of interviews allowed me to conclude that salespeople tended to feel a closer bond with their brand if they came from the same culture or country. Salespeople from France naturally tend to identify strongly with French luxury brands such as Dior, Chanel, or Lancôme, since they feel culturally close to the brand. The label "Made in France" makes them extremely proud. They feel as if they are contributing to their beloved country's well-being and economic development. It is just the same with Italians serving and advocating for Italian fashion brands such as Prada, Miu Miu or Fendi. Feeling close to a brand can also be triggered if a brand's origin corresponds to your own culture or if a head office is close to where you grew up. This might lead to the impression of being born in the same place and shapes a certain familiarity between the salesperson and the brand.

> *I have been working for Lancôme for 17 years and it is a true love story which began very early. When I was ten years old, I said to my mum that I wanted to work in cosmetics. This was because we were living close to Chevilly-Larue, where the brand Lancôme was created by Arnaud Petitjean. My mum was surprised to hear that a child of my age could be so definite with regard to her future professional dream. Usually, at this*

age, kids want to become veterinarians. I was passionate about cosmet-
ics, and Lancôme in particular. Therefore, it was natural to apply to work
for this brand after my studies.

(Sandrine Sabathé, Sales Representative at Lancôme)

Finding the perfect match between salespeople and the brand they represent is important as it increases the chances of strong brand loyalty. Salespeople feel comfortable when they get the impression that they are understood, in the right place, and that they do not need to change their character in order to fit in.

I tried several times to attract salespeople who worked for Prada to Sonia
Rykiel, but I noticed that it was simply impossible to do so. Their values
were so bound in with their brand's values that you could not tear them
away. It was not at all a money issue. It was because the values of both
brands are not the same at all. I strongly believe that the first motivation to
serve a brand is not money but the values that make the brand so special.

(Shayda de Bary, Store Manager at Sonia Rykiel,
former Store Manager for Dries Van Noten and Miu Miu)

Matching values have another big advantage. The more salespeople identify with a brand's values, the more easily they can transfer these values to their customers. And customers who identify with their brand are willing to spend a fortune on it.

Even if you get the impression that your candidate matches your brand's identity perfectly, you also need to find the perfect match in terms of sales channels. Not all salespeople are equally adapted to working in a stand-alone boutique or in a department store. During my interviews, I met both types. They were usually quite polarized and preferred one model to the other. I rarely encountered salespeople who were keen on working in different sales channels. It is therefore important for recruiters to find out if candidates are better suited to the working style of department stores, where there is a high volume of people traffic, a lot of noise, many brands represented, more people looking rather than buying and a very curious multinational customer base, or if they would prefer working in a stand-alone boutique. In the latter shopping environment, the salesperson needs to fully embody the spirit of luxury, be very focused on service, and be able to maintain an excellent relationship with the customer and expand the customer base continuously. In contrast to department stores, the atmosphere is calm, there is less traffic, but the brand environment is exclusively yours. When young salespeople start, it is always good training to have them experience both environments to see where they feel most comfortable.

5.3   Diversity over monotony

Brands that assemble their sales teams in a rather heterogeneous way favor diversity over monotony and have a greater chance of strengthening their relationship with their salespeople as the brand environment becomes more exciting, dynamic and colorful. Salespeople generally tend to seek movement instead of stillness and repetition. The way you compose your teams can therefore contribute to creating positive and naturally dynamic stores.

Besides, diversity reflects the reality of your customer base. Today, boundaries are fading, customers travel and people are not tied to one store, city or country. Thousands of people migrate and move from one place to another. Therefore, customers change constantly and are becoming increasingly international. In luxury, especially, there are certain emerging cultures such as the Chinese or Russians, where the hunger for luxury is huge. Your brands must adapt to this shift. It becomes crucial to hire people within your teams who are familiar with these cultures and can serve customers in their respective languages.

Diversity can smooth out tensions. It opens up our minds, allowing us to learn from each other, to discover new behavior and to question our own. This openness and self-awareness are important elements in a salesperson's progression and growth. By observing colleagues from different cultures, salespeople also develop a better understanding of their customers' diversity. By expanding their own horizons, salespeople will become more flexible when interacting with their environment. They will also become more receptive to change and better accept new input from brand management.

So how can diversity in a sales team be expressed and achieved?

- Try to integrate different cultures within your team. If possible, chose cultures that also reflect your customer base.
- Try to find an equal balance between men and women. This helps to avoid unnecessary tensions, which may come up if too many men or women are working closely together.

- Mix up different age groups, since customers usually feel confident with people of their own age.
- Compose your team by integrating various profiles from different professional backgrounds and experiences. This allows salespeople to learn from each other, to benefit from mutual experiences and expertise, and allows everyone to grow.
- Make sure that your teams rotate between stores and that they become familiar with different types of sales environments. Alternatively, you can compose a small team of salespeople that hop from door to door while others stay in one place. In order to favor the relationship-building factor for your brand, you should always pay attention to the person's character to decide upon the role he or she plays in the store.

FIG 26 Fostering team spirit and brand relationships through diversity

Salespeople should never be sad. They need to feel pleasure in what they are doing. The best method here is to mix your teams in the most diverse way: you need to mix the young and the old, men and women, people of all religions and various backgrounds. If you manage to compose your team in a way that reflects social diversity, it will be easier for your team to feel the joy and the fun that goes with the demanding daily tasks asked of a salesperson.

(Christian Blanckaert, Professor in Luxury Management at ESCP Europe and former CEO of Hermès Sellier and Hermès International)

Our sales teams are even more closely related to each other and to the brand now that we have started integrating diverse profiles in terms of professional experience and backgrounds. We have former actors and writers but also future fragrance creators. This diversity nourishes salespeople and comes through in the way they approach customers, explain the products and understand the brand. Juliette, for instance, is a blogger and has an amazing capacity to distinguish fragrances. I put her in a moving sales position, which means that she rotates between our different points of sale. This adds dynamism and strengthens the ties between our stores. I noticed that the fixed sales advisors love asking her a lot of questions when she comes, since she writes a blog about fragrances. She brings a breath of fresh air, which is good for the brand. Relationships are much more balanced and natural. Diversity can also be achieved by mixing cultures, since each person brings along a new sales approach. For instance, I am currently integrating a Japanese fragrance creator, who studied fragrance design in Tokyo. I think that it will be very interesting and enriching for our sales advisors to have her in their team.

(Sylvie Coumau, General Manager of Editions de Parfums Frédéric Malle)

Conclusion

The five Olympic rings of sales force–brand relationships allowed us to get to the heart of salespeople's motivation and personality, as they revealed how close they felt toward the brand they represented. In numerous quotes, salespeople shared what made it possible for them to develop strong emotional ties with their brands:

- Why they fell in love with the brand.
- Why they could identify with it.
- Why they decided to trust the brand.
- Why they felt so proud of it.
- What gave them the recognition to feel close to the brand and hold on to it.

Based on my results from intense interviews with top managers and salespeople, I then developed 18 heart-winning strategies, which together can be described by the term Luxury Relationship Branding Strategies. They can be seen as recipes for all managers who want salespeople to develop close relationships with their brand and become its most enthusiastic ambassadors. The ingredients are perfectly adapted to those who want to kindle a passion in the hearts of salespeople, those who want to avoid losing their precious people to a higher paying competitor and those who want to create more stability within the corporation in the long run.

In times when the economic and social environment is fragile, when rules and habits are constantly changing, when new business models are emerging, it is important to strengthen your company with human values. Money is not always the best solution in times when, even in business, people are seeking for a deeper sense of fulfillment.

- The game is over for old-school management techniques that thrive on elbow grease and ego-boosting principles.
- The game is over for "Bribery Management" based on the ideology of "I pay, you do."
- The game is over for "Dictator Management" based on the idea of "I say, you do."
- The game is over for "Slavery Management," which follows the creed of "You are mine, so do what I say."

All of these management schools have been widespread and are unfortunately still active in many companies. None of them are able to generate a passionate and motivated sales force. Don't even think about creating close ties with your people if these are the criteria upon which your firm's employee–employer relationships are based.

It is time to give way to new management styles that are based on human values, a strong community spirit, a sense of participation and fluid 360-degree exchange. This is a management style in which salespeople are at the heart of the company, where they are fully integrated and interact with all services and departments, and are thus influenced and inspired by the expertise and talent of all the employees that make up the rich diversity of your company. Develop a strong sense of service even within your corporation: where departments serve other departments in the best possible way in order to help each other prepare to confront the competitor and serve the client. Salespeople become the clients of top management, human resources, marketing, finance, communication, merchandising, product development and logistics. This makes sense since their profession is among the most diverse and complex within the entire organization. Salespeople need the tools to be knowledgeable about the brand and feel comfortable selling it. This sense of service is the basis for mutual respect, higher transparency, greater efficiency, better results and, above all, the emergence of emotional ties between salespeople, their brand and the entire organization. All are related and connected.

As opposed to the previously mentioned management styles, I want to call this new approach the "We-Management" Strategy.

This strategy, which fits perfectly in modern times, can be illustrated by the "sunshine model" and stands in contrast to the "raindrop model."

The latter sees the salesperson as being the last element in the chain or the last drop that pours down from the sky before falling onto the hard ground of reality. The salesperson is the last one to touch the soil before bursting as he interacts with an increasingly demanding customer. If raindrops pour too heavily, floods can't be avoided. This situation would be a disaster for every brand.

In order to prevent brands from such hard landings and unnecessarily flooded grounds, the "Sunshine Model" builds a solid base, provides sales people with the tools to deal with reality and strengthens brands in the long run. In this configuration, all departments provide relevant information to the sales force and are willing to share their expertise. At the same time, salespeople nourish the experts with ongoing information from the field since they are at the front line. This helps all departments to move ahead hand in hand with the sales force, and to be perfectly informed with

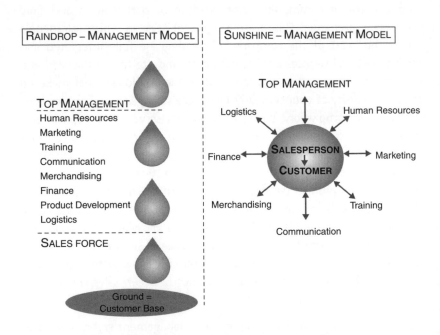

FIG 27 / The Raindrop and the Sunshine Management Models

regard to the market reality. Exchanging mutual information across departments and hierarchy levels keeps all employees on board (Figure 27).

Let me use the image of the sales manager's boat, to which I referred at the beginning of the book. What kind of boat do we need in order to win the race against other ships navigating the same rough ocean filled with surprises and dangers? How must this ship be organized, built and guided?

The vessel that was drawn at the beginning of this book was a luxury ferry, which moved ahead thanks to the rowing sales force at the bottom of the boat. Top management appeared several levels higher, far away on the luxurious upper deck, guiding the ship but not necessarily caring about the rowing crowd.

Is this the kind of ship that allows you to win the race against all the other vessels that are out there in the ocean? Is this the organization you need in order to hold your teams together, motivate them to go on even if the waves are high and the storm is strong? Probably not!

If you want to win the race, you better have a streamlined sailing boat allowing you to sail close to the wind, and be flexible enough to change direction quickly if necessary, smoothly adjusting to the waves as you move at high speed. Everyone is on deck, at the same level, placed at a dedicated post where each team member is at their best and knows exactly what to do in each situation. They form a team and help each other excel. The captain is at the helm. He preserves the global vision toward the final destination; he keeps an eye on each person and motivates everyone to keep going. All team members feel strongly attached to their sailboat and to each other. They want to win the race together as a family, with common goals and aspirations.

ILL 22 / **Winning the brand regatta**

(Source: Albert Dessinateur for Michaela Merk)

Bibliography

Aaker, D. (1991) *Managing Brand Equity: Capitalizing on the Value of a Brand Name*. New York: The Free Press.

Aaker, D. (1996) "Measuring brand equity across products and markets." *California Management Review*, 38(3), 102–19.

Aaker, D. (2003) "The power of the branded differentiator." *MIT Sloan Management Review* (Fall), 83–7.

Aaker, J. (1997) "Dimensions of brand personality." *Journal of Marketing Research*, 34 (August), 347–57.

Adkins, R. T. (1979) "Evaluating and comparing salesmen's performance." *Industrial Marketing Management*, 8 (June), 207–12.

Ahearne, M., A. Rapp, D. Hughes and R. Jindal (2010) "Managing sales force product perceptions and control systems in the success of new product introductions." *Journal of Marketing Research*, 47, 764–76.

Ahearne, M., A. Rapp, B. J. Mariadoss, and S. Ganesan (2012) "Challenges of CRM implementation in business-to-business markets: a contingency perspective." *Journal of Personal Selling and Sales Management*, 117–29.

Akremi, A. et al. (2009) "Rôle de la reconnaissance dans la construction de l'identité au travail." *Relations Industrielles*, 64(4), 662–84.

Albert, N., D. R. Merunka and P. Vallette-Florence (2008) "Conceptualizing and measuring consumers' love towards their brands." *Society for Marketing Advances Proceedings* (January), 108–11.

Allen, N. J. and J. P. Meyer (1990) "The measurement and antecedents of affective, continuance and normative commitment." *Journal of Occupational Psychology*, 63, 1–18.

Amabile, T. M., K. G. Hill, B. A. Hennessey and E. M. Tighe (1994) "The work preference inventory: assessing intrinsic and extrinsic motivational orientations." *Journal of Personality and Social Psychology*, 66 (November), 930–67.

Anderson, E. and R. L. Oliver (1987) "Perspectives on behavior-based versus outcome-based sales force control systems." *Journal of Marketing*, 51(4), 76–88.

Bain & Company (2013) *Worldwide Luxury Market Monitor*, Spring.

Beltramini, F. F. and K. R. Evans (1988) "Salesperson motivation to perform and job satisfaction: a sales contest participant perspective." *Journal of Personal Selling and Sales Management*, 8, 35–42.

Berry, L. L. (2007) "The best companies are generous companies." *Business Horizons* 50, 263–9.

Blackston, M. (1992) "Observations: building brand equity by managing the brand's relationships." *Journal of Advertising Research* (May/June), 79–83.

Blackston, M. (1993) "Beyond brand personality: building brand relationships." In: D. Aaker and A. Biel, *Brand Equity and Advertising: Advertising's Role in Building Strong Brands*. Hillsdale, NI: Erlbaum, 113–24.

Brun, J. P. and N. Dugas (2008) "An analysis of employee recognition: perspectives on human resources practices." *The International Journal of Human Resource Management*, 19(4), 716–30.

Burmann, C. and S. Zeplin (2005) "Building brand commitment: a behavioral approach to internal brand management." *Journal of Brand Management*, 12(4), 279–300.

Chandy, R. K. and G. J. Tellis (1998) "Organizing for radical product innovation: the overlooked role of willingness to cannibalize." *Journal of Marketing Research*, 35(4), 474–87.

Chaudhuri, A. and M. Holbrook (2001) "The chain of effects from brand trust and brand affect to brand performance: the role of brand loyalty." *Journal of Marketing*, 65, 81–93.

Chaudhuri, A. and M. Holbrook (2002) "Product-class effects on brand commitment and brand outcomes: the role of brand trust and brand affect." *Brand Management*, 10(1), 33–58.

Chonko, L. B. (1986) "Organizational commitment in the sales force." *Journal of Personal Selling & Management*, 6, 19–27.

Churchill Jr., G. A., N. M. Ford, S. W. Hartley and O. C. Walker Jr. (1985) "The determinants of salesperson performance: a meta-analysis." *Journal of Marketing Research*, 22, 103–18.

Churchill Jr., G. A., N. M. Ford, S. W. Hartley and O. C. Walker (1993) *Sales Force Management: Planning, Implementation and Control* (4th edn.). Homewood, IL: Richard D.Irwin, Inc.

Cravens, D. W., T. N. Ingram, R. W. LaForge and C. E. Young (1993) "Behavior-based and outcome-based salesforce control systems." *Journal of Marketing*, 57 (October), 47–59.

Cron, W. L. (1984) "Industrial salesperson development: a career stages perspective." *Journal of Marketing*, 48 (Fall), 41–52.

Cron, W. L., A. J. Dubinsky and R. E. Michaels (1988) "The influence of career stages on components of salesperson motivation." *Journal of Marketing*, 52, 78–92.

Darwin, C. ([1872] 1998) *The Expression of the Emotions in Man and Animals* (3rd edn.). New York: Oxford University Press.

C. Droge, J. T. Mentzer and M. B. Myers (2009) "Creating committment and loyalty behavior among retailers: what are the roles of service quality and satisfaction?" *Journal of the Academy of Marketing Science*, 37, 440–54.

C. Moorman, R. Deshpadé and G. Zaltman (1993) "Factors affecting trust in market research relationships." *Journal of Marketing*, 57 (January), 81–101.

Deci, E. L. (1971) "Effects of externally mediated rewards on intrinsic motivation." *Journal of Personal and Social Psychology*, 18, 105–15.

Drigotas, S. M. and C. E. Rusbult (1992) "Should I stay or should I go? A dependence model of breakups." *Journal of Personality and Social Psychology*, 62 (January), 62–87.

Eisenberger, R. et al. (1999) "Does pay for performance increase or decrease perceived self-determination and intrinsic motivation?" *Journal of Personality and Social Psychology*, 77 (5), 1026–40.

Flaherty, T. B. and J. M. Pappas (2000) "The role of trust in salesperson–sales manager relationships." *Journal of Personal Selling and Sales Management*, 20 (Fall), 271–8.

Fournier, S. (1998) "Consumers and their brands: developing relationship theory in consumer research." *Journal of Consumer Research*, 24, 343–73.

Futrell, C. M. (1979) "Measurement of salespeople's job satisfaction: convergent and discripinant validity of corresponding INDESALES and job descriptive index scales." *Journal of Marketing Research*, 16 (November), 594–7.

Futrell, C. M. and Parasuraman, A. (1984) "The relationship of satisfaction and performance to salesforce turnover." *Journal of Marketing*, 48, 33–40.

Gilmore, G. W. (1919) *Animism*. Boston, MA: Marshall Jones.

Herzberg, F., B. Mausner and B. Snyderman (1959) *The Motivation to Work*. New York: Wiley.

Hinde, Robert A. (1979) *Towards Understanding Relationships*. London: Academy Press.

Hughes, D. E. and M. Ahearne (2010) "Energizing the reseller's sales force: the power of brand identification." *Journal of Marketing*, 74, 81–96.

Hultink, E. J., E. J. Atuahene-Gima Hultink and K. Atuahene-Gima (2000) "The effect of sales force adoption on new product selling performance." *Journal of Product Innovation Management*, 17, 435–50.

Hunt, S. D., L. B. Chonko and R. Van Wood (1985) "Organizational commitment and marketing." *Journal of Marketing* (Winter), 112–26.

Ingram, T. N., K. S. Lee and S. J. Skinner (1989) "An empirical assessment of salesperson motivation, commitment and job outcomes." *Journal of Personal Selling and Sales Management*, 9, 25–33.

Jacobs, R. (2003) "Turn employees into brand ambassadors." *ABA Bank Marketing*, 35(3), 22–6.

Jacobson, R. and D. A. Aaker (1987) "The strategic role of product quality." *Journal of Marketing*, 51 (October), 31–44.

Jacoby, J. and R. Chestnut (1978) *Brand Loyalty Measurement and Management*. New York: John Wiley.

Jaworski, B. and A. Kohli (1991) "Supervisory feedback: alternative types and their impact on salespeople's performance and satisfaction." *Journal of Marketing Research*, 28, 191–201.

Jobber, D. and R. Lee (1994) "A comparison of the perceptions of sales management and salespeople towards sales force motivation and demotivation." *Journal of Marketing Management*, 10, 325–32.

Kapferer, J-N. (2007) *Les marques, Capital de l'entreprise, Groupe Eyrolles* (4th edn.).

Kelley, H. H. and J. W. Thibaut (1978) *Interpersonal Relationships: A Theory of Interdependence*. New York: Wiley.

Kim, W. Chan and R. Mauborgne (1997) "Value innovation: the strategic logic of high growth." *Harvard Business Review*, 75(1), 103–12.

McAlexander, J., J. Schouten and H. Koenig (2002) "Building brand community." *Journal of Marketing*, 66(1), 38–54.

McCracken, G. (1989) "Who is the celebrity endorser? Cultural foundations of the endorsement process." *Journal of Consumer Research*, 16 (December), 310–21.

McDougall, W. (1911) *Body and Mind: A History and Defense of Animism*. New York: Macmillan.

Merk, M. (2012) "Strengthening sales force–brand relationships: a new management strategy for retailers?" PhD Thesis, Sorbonne Business School, October.

Merk, M. (2013) "Appréhender la relation marque-vendeur comme un facteur de motivation." In: G. Michel, *Management transversal de la marque*. Paris: Dunod.

Meyer, J. P. et al. (2004) "Employee commitment and motivation: a conceptual analysis and integrative model." *Journal of Applied Psychology*, 89(6), 991–1007.

Michel, G. (2009) *Au coeur de la marque: Les clés du management de la marque*. Paris: Dunod.

Morgan, R. M. and S. D. Hunt (1994) "The commitment–trust theory of relationship marketing." *Journal of Marketing*, 58, 20–38.

Perlman, D. and B. Fehr (1987) "The development of intimate relationships." In: D. Perlman and S. Duck, *Intimate Relationships Development, Dynamics, and Deterioration*. Newbury Park, CA: Sage, 13–42.

Porter, L. W. and E. E. Lawler (1968) *Managerial Attitudes and Performance*. Homewood, IL: Richard D. Irwin, Inc.

Punjaisri, K. and A. Wilson (2007) "The role of internal branding in the delivery of employee brand promise." *Journal of Brand Management*, 15(1), 57–70.

Ramlall, S. (2004) "A review of employee motivation theories and their implications for employee retention within organizations." *The Journal of American Academy of Business*, 5(1), 52–63.

Rapaille, G. C. (2006) "Leveraging the psychology of the salesperson." *Harvard Business Review* (July–August), 42–7.

Rochford, L. and T. R. Wotruba (1996) "The impact of sales management changes on new product success." *Journal of Academy of Marketing Science*, 24(3), 263–70.

Rubin, Z. (1973) *Liking and Loving: An Invitation to Social Psychology*. New York: Holt, Rinehart & Winston.

Singh, J. and G. K. Rhoads (1997) "Boundary role ambiguity in marketing-oriented positions: a multidimensional, multifaceted operationalization." *Journal of Marketing Research*, 28, 328–38.

Stanton, W. J., R. H. Buskirk and R. Spiro (1991) *Management of a Sales Force*. Boston, MA: Irwin.

Steenburgh, T. and M. Ahearne (2012) "Motivating salespeople: what really works." *Harvard Business Review* (July–August), 70–5.

Stipek, D., S. Recchia and S. McClintic (1992) "Self-evaluation in young children." *Monographs of the Society for Research in Child Development*, 57(1) (serial no. 226).

Tajfel, H. (1978) "The achievement of group differentiation." In: H. Tajfel, *Differentiation between Social Groups: Studies in the Social Psychology of Intergroup Relations*. London: Academic Press, 77–98.

Taylor, C. (1994) "The politics of recognition." In: A. Gutmann, *Multiculturalism*. Princeton, NJ: Princeton University Press, 25–73.

Tosti, T. and D. Stotz (2001) "Brand: building your brand from the inside out." *Marketing Management*, 10(2), 28–33.

Tracy, J. L. and R. W. Robins (2004) "Show your pride: evidence for a discrete emotion expression." *Psychological Science*, 15, 194–7.

Tsang, N. K. F. et al. (2011) "An examination of the relationship between employee perception and hotel brand equity." *Journal of Travel & Tourism Marketing*, 28, 281–497.

Tuner, J. H. (2009) "Measuring turnover: a review of traditional measurement methods and development of measurement techniques based on survival analysis." *Proceedings of the Academy of Marketing Studies*, 14(1), 59–64.

Tyagi, P. K. (1990) "Inequities in organizations, salesperson motivation and job satisfaction." *International Journal of Research in Marketing* (December), 135–48.

Wallendorf, M. and E. Arnould (1989) "My favorite things: a cross-cultural inquiry into object attachment, possessiveness, and social linkage." *Journal of Consumer Research*, 14, 531–47.

Weitz, B. A. and K. D. Bradford (1999) "Personal selling and sales management: a relationship marketing perspective." *Journal of the Academy of Marketing Science*, 27(2), 241–54.

Subject Index

Name Index

Brand Index

Printed and bound by CPI Group (UK) Ltd, Croydon, CR0 4YY